YESTERDAY'S TODAYS

- A STORY OF SURVIVAL AGAINST THE ODDS

Anneliese Johnson

Yesterday's Todays

Anneliese Johnson

1889 books

Yesterday's Todays

Copyright © Anneliese Johnson 2023

All rights reserved. The moral rights
of the author have been asserted.
Cover artwork © 1889 books

Photographs copyright © Anneliese Johnson 2023,
except:
public domain photograph of Treblinka II burning
taken by Franciszek Ząbecki, eye witness to every
Holocaust transport that came into the camp,
and public domain photograph of Eisenach Synagogue.
Dedication panel border image by kjpargeter on Freepik.

www.1889books.co.uk
ISBN: 978-1-915045-28-7

For Margarete, David and Lawrence

CONTENTS

Map of Places Mentioned

Preface	1
Chapter 1: Krakow	3
Chapter 2: A New Home in Eisenach	7
Chapter 3: The Early Days of the War	18
Chapter 4: The Fear Grows	38
Chapter 5: The Gates of Hell	54
Chapter 6: My Homecoming	64
Chapter 7: Reunion	77
Chapter 8: The Turning Point, Summer 1945	89
Chapter 9: Decision Time	89
Chapter 10: Farewell to the East	103
Chapter 11: My Return to the East	111
Chapter 12: My First Taste of Freedom	126
Chapter 13: A New Life in Sheffield, England	137
Bonus Chapter: Lottie's Story	148

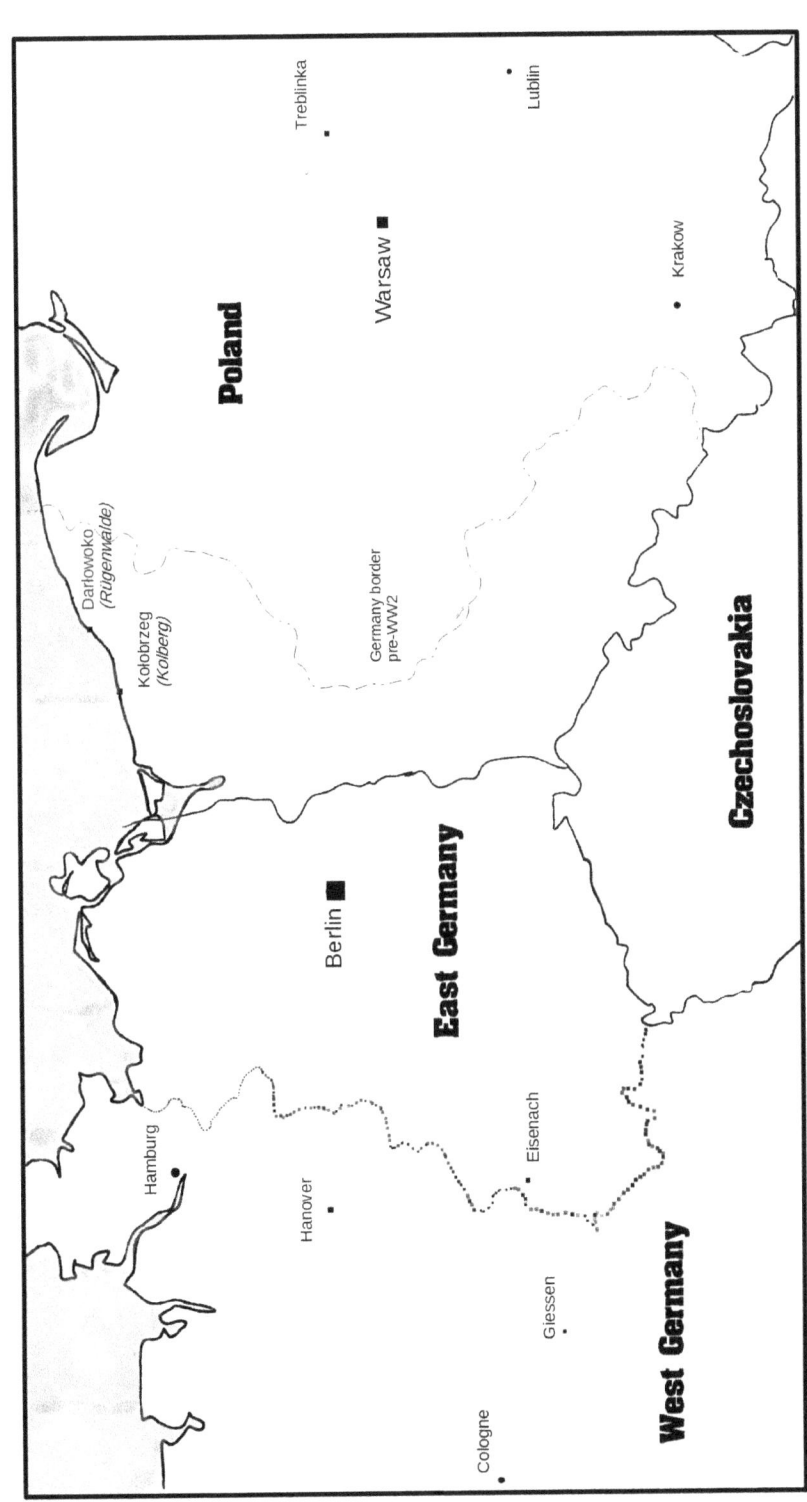

Preface

Anneliese Johnson is believed to be the last survivor of the Treblinka death camp, escaping during the uprising of August 1943.

Treblinka camp was one of the main sites for the carrying out of the Nazis' co-called "final-solution." Some were forced into labour, being told they would be spared, but they knew that only prolonged their lives for a short time. In the uprising, prisoners seized weapons, set camp buildings on fire and made an assault on the main gate under machine-gun fire from the guards. 840 people were believed to be in the camp when the uprising took place. Of those, 100 or so were incapable of assisting, and around 200 made it out, half of whom were recaptured and killed.

Only around 80-90 people survived; their stories, like Anneliese's, bare valuable insights into what happened in the camp – part of our collective responsibility to remember.

Yesterday's Todays was a long time in the making. Anneliese started committing her story to paper in the 1990s, using her diary to recall the shocking and remarkable events of her life. She self-published the first edition in 2020. Anneliese would like to thank her friend Rose for her help. She has also had help with compiling and editing her story from Max Munday and Nick Lampert, volunteers at the Association of Jewish Refugees. She would also like to thank Chris Tweddle for this help and support.

This revised edition, published by 1889 Books, contains additional material, especially from chapter 11 onwards and a new chapter 13 covering Anneliese's life in England in more detail. Some extra photographs have been included and certain errors in the first edition have been corrected.

Anneliese also wrote an account of her friend Lottie's survival story. This was originally going to be part of a new book, but it made more sense to revise *Yesterday's Todays* and to include *Lottie's Story* as a bonus chapter.

Anneliese's Diary

– **1889 Books, November 2023**

Chapter 1
Krakow

Krakow was the royal capital for half a millennium and has witnessed and absorbed more of Polish history than any other country. No other city in Poland has so many historic buildings and monuments. Krakow is the city with character and soul. According to legend, there lived a wise and powerful prince, called Krak or Krakus, who built, on a hill, a castle named Krakus and founded a town after himself, Krakow. This is where I was born in 1929 and lived until a decision was reached to leave the country to make a new start.

My father, Kurt Wegner, was born in Rügenwalde (Darłowko), on the south coast of the Baltic Sea. Rügenwalde was a seaside town in the west Pomeranian region. My father, as a young man took up his studies at the University of Hamburg. He remained in Hamburg to take up his first gainful employment with an export and import agency. He often had to travel to other countries on business and financial matters. On one occasion he was sent to Poland, Krakow. It was there that he met a young lady, who was later to become his wife, and my mother. My father settled in Krakow for a few years, I think, where he worked. These were happy times for them, the sun always seemed to shine, and the world was always smiling and happy.

My maternal grandparents' jewellery shop in Kolberg

Their life was about to be shattered. The signs of war had been slowly and ominously becoming more apparent with the passing years. It was only when Hitler became Chancellor in 1933, on Hindenburg's death, when, for us, the good times began to recede, and people really started to worry about the future. The Nuremburg Laws were introduced and these certainly threatened some Jews, as well as Gentiles. It was a forewarning that they would consider fleeing the gathering storm. My mother, Erna Blankenburg, was Jewish, but my father was "Aryan." My father's father suggested to come back to Kołobrzeg as he was retiring and offered the business to my father. It was a confectionary shop, also selling tea and coffee. My father accepted.

My grandparents' Villa in Kolberg.

Soon we were all on our way to Pomerania, where my parents and grandparents felt more secure. After a few years, uneasiness was felt by my parents as the Nazis started to look for "non-Aryans." But since my father was an "Aryan" they felt safer and believed that they could get out of the situation. My parents got a lawyer who gave us new identities. But they helped only regarding our nationalities, namely from Polish to German, as we were now on German soil.

Although they had happy times in Krakow, my parents realised that bad times were approaching. Wartime in Poland lasted longer than for any other country in Europe. Between the commencement of the Nazi attack at dawn on 1st September 1939 and the final capitulation of the Nazi Reich on VE Day, on the 9th May 1945, there stretched over two thousand days of violence and suffering. In proportion to its size, Poland incurred more damage and casualties than any other country on Earth. Without cannon, without swords, but through faith alone the Lord God shall conquer on our behalf.

Kołobrzeg had no industry and consequently the air was healthy, invigorating and pollution free. It was a beautiful resort nestling like a jewel on the Baltic coastline, washed by an ever-moving sea and backed by the richly fertile province of Pomerania which spread out invitingly behind it in to the very heart of Poland. During the period between the wars, visitors of all nationalities were attracted to its amenities, and it became the playground not just for Europeans but also for rich Americans. It was a place for relaxation, pleasure, freedom, happiness, and a happy childhood for my sister and me. Kołobrzeg has not always been a haven of tranquillity and rest, however, having been subjected to a somewhat chequered and violent history. Through the centuries, Kolberg, as it was originally known, has been fought over repeatedly by neighbouring countries.

My maternal grandparents in 1930

Happy times before everything changed

Chapter 2
A New Home in Eisenach

It was the spring of 1938, when I was 8 years old, that my parents, Jutta and I finally left Kołobrzeg. It was a very sad and emotional occasion as the actual time of departure approached, because we were leaving behind my beloved grandparents and all our dear friends, and venturing forth into the relative unknown, not knowing when we might see them all again. I am sure it must have been even harder for my parents who had lived so much of their lives in Kołobrzeg building up a reputation, earning the respect of the community and becoming pillars of its society. For Jutta and me however, although Kołobrzeg was all we had ever known, our departure was viewed more as an adventurous escapade, our youth and our parents shielding us from the seriousness of our situation. Nonetheless, the whole family was apprehensive at the big step on which we had decided to embark in our search for a better and safer life. With war clouds gathering over Europe, my parents must have had considerable fortitude and not a little courage, uprooting themselves and their family in such treacherous times.

My grandmother, mother, sister and me

With hindsight, the situation in Kołobrzeg must have been far worse than we two young girls believed as it drove our mother and father to sell everything and embark upon this drastic and dramatic move into the German heartland – but then they told us we were leaving because I needed a change of air to combat the chronic catarrh which had been affecting my health more recently.

My paternal granparents in 1918

My parents went ahead to purchase a house and shop and generally organise the move, so Jutta and I resided with our grandparents for a short time, after which they also left Krakow. After my parents had been in Eisenach for a couple of months it was considered time for us to join them and accordingly my mother came to fetch us.

We boarded the train which was to take us to our new life and a number of my parent's closer friends came to bid us farewell. The journey would take several hours and as Jutta and I pressed our noses against the glass, the clouds of acrid smoke billowing forth from the funnel of our steam engine lay incongruously across the plain of Pomerania which was passing by so seductively in the early spring sunshine just beyond our carriage window. Slowly, the flatlands were replaced by an undulating countryside of mountains and dales, rivers and lakes, and the castles of which fairy tales are made. It was beautiful to behold and a totally new experience for Jutta and me. There were forests of dark green pine trees stretching out for miles and rushing torrents of bouncing white water

Father and mother in 1921

tumbling and spilling from the hills into azure blue lakes. We could see clearly for ourselves why so many poets had written so eloquently and lyrically of here, called Thüringen, Germany. Jutta and I leaned out of the window so that we could see more clearly and we chatted incessantly as each new marvel unfolded before our eyes. The clattering wheels of our intrusive transportation, and the labouring chuffs and piercing hisses of escaping steam from the hardworking engine as it struggled up a particularly obtrusive incline, could not detract from the natural beauty of the rolling landscape so new to us two girls.

The train stopped here and there to set down passengers or to pick up new ones, sometimes in quaint little hamlets where there might be only a couple of farmsteads and a few farm workers' houses and, at other times, in a busy metropolis where everything was bustling in a hive of feverish activity. And all the while Jutta and I would chatter on, remarking about the unusual outfit someone was wearing, wondering what sort of life certain of our fellow travellers might be following, where they might be going and such other fantasising that comes from excited minds nurtured by novel and thought-evoking stimuli.

All the trains I had known up until then always seemed to find the whole business of moving from here to there a strenuously laborious effort, and this was no exception. It would roll into a station amid a series of jerks and shudders presumably to ensure no-one slept through their intended destination, smoke and steam enveloping the immediate area in a clinging carbon fog which an insensitive nose could detect on ones clothes for several hours afterwards, and that distinctive aroma associated with all steam trains would pervade the nostrils. I always used to consider it was not a particularly clean form of travel, a thought reinforced by present day attitudes towards pollution, but it had a passion and romanticism not encountered in other forms of transportation. After a period at the platform while the engine quietly hissed and grumbled as it contemplated the practicalities of moving off again, there would suddenly be a rapid ejection of steam and two quick blasts on the whistle, followed closely by the noise of huffing and puffing as clouds of black smoke belched skywards in such profusion that even a short-sighted North American could have read its message from ten miles away. Then with much juddering and shaking of its passengers, the train would endeavour to pick up speed as gracefully as possible. The engines of those days had a certain majesty and an aura of unsurpassed power as they raced across the landscape scattering all before them, but they were not well suited to frequent stopping and starting, and seemed to lose much of their brooding menace as they tried with slipping wheels and a certain impropriety to ease their way embarrassingly, even apologetically one might say, out of each station.

Our train stopped for some time in Erfurt, Thüringen, and from there, it was only a few more short hauls to our ultimate destination, Eisenach. The town of Eisenach is a cultural centre situated in the Western half of the province of Thüringen. It has a renowned history, which largely revolves around its castle, the famous Wartburg. Even today's tourists flock in their thousands from all over the world to visit Wartburg, where Martin Luther translated the New Testament into German. As the train made its final approach and settled for us to alight with comfort onto the platform, amidst swirling clouds of steam and smoke, the excitement felt by us all rose inwardly as we responded to the station's bustle and activity invading our privacy. We had arrived and, for better or worse, there was no going back now.

Jutta and me

Outside the station a shining black carriage with a beautiful brown horse drawn to it, was waiting for us. We climbed aboard, bouncing excitedly on the plush leather seats while my mother saw that our luggage was properly stowed, and then the jolly driver, whistling gaily as his horse trotted along, transported us over the cobblestones to our new home. A housemaid was already there waiting to greet us and, after the formalities of introduction were over, Jutta and I dashed off to explore while the grown-ups busied themselves around the house. My father had sold both his confectionary shops in Kołobrzeg and had bought just one in Eisenach into which my parents intended to plough their joint efforts so that it might develop and expand more rapidly. The shop and our new house were some distance apart and consequently, a housemaid had been engaged to look after Jutta and me in order that my parents would have greater freedom and could devote extra time in pursuit of their business endeavours.

I was disappointed that my father had not been able to meet us at Eisenach station, but my mother explained that he had many pressing duties at the shop and, with uncertainty over the duration of our journey, because timetables were fairly meaningless in those days, he could not afford to waste valuable hours waiting needlessly our arrival. When he did return to our new home that evening however, we were overjoyed to see him, flinging our arms around him and regaling him with our excited chatter. We were delighted to be reunited as a family once again and any reservations that might have lurked in the recesses of our being were driven out by the reassuring presence of my father. We hugged and kissed him and gave him our news from the two months separation. We then had a little family party to celebrate, and retired to our bed later than usual, exhausted by the long day's exertions.

Although the duties of the maid included caring for Jutta and me, it was my mother who accompanied us to our new school each morning until we had grown accustomed to the route. It entailed a walk of several miles each day, being a much longer journey than in Kołobrzeg, and convenient buses and trams were few and far between. Indeed, our new school did not stand on any direct bus or tram route, and it was only people who could afford a horse and carriage who were able to venture off the beaten track and live even further afield. We were not accustomed to the hilly nature of our new surroundings either, and the steep track up to the school I found particularly arduous. In winter it could become especially treacherous and slippery, and I used to dread the walk back down the hill after school in the depth of the winter when snow and ice were around. I soon made friends, a fairly easy undertaking when one is young, and it was not long before I grew acclimatised to the people, the children, and their practices, which were so very different to those I'd known in Pomerania. The Polish and German interface within a relaxed Kołobrzeg culture had been replaced by a much stricter Germanic doctrine and ideology.

Hitler somehow seemed to have persuaded much of the populace to relinquish many of their freedoms and to quieten the occasional disapproving voice of their conscience. The boys had their hair clipped to a uniform shortness, the girls invariably cultivated massive plaits to be like each other, and the adults paraded every Sunday like so many satisfied corpulent penguins as they strutted their way for 'kaffee und kuchen' at relatives or friends houses, always clutching the customary bunch of flowers. At the drop of a hat however, or the most incidental of triggers such as a raised voice, this acquiescent crowd could suddenly be transformed into a baying jostling mob, with eyes ablaze with nationalistic fervour and right arms outstretched. By providing work for the unemployed, an army for his generals and playing upon the indignities of the conquered peoples, particularly among his disenchanted middle classes, and also of course not forgetting the threat of detention camps for those who showed

A Nazi parade through the streets, taken from the upstairs of our shop on Johannistrasse

dissent, Hitler had demonstrated how well he understood the German peoples and had chanced his luck with a disconsolate nation looking for improvement.

My upbringing had shielded me to a very large extent from the hardships out of which the Hitler rollercoaster had been spawned, but with our family's move to Eisenach, I was conscious even at my tender years of a significant cultural change to that which I had become accustomed. There were many lovely hot sunny days during the summers of 1938 and 1939, and our teacher often took us out into the countryside to further our studies. Trips were planned in advance and we all participated eagerly in their preparation and execution. Such excursions were most enjoyable diversions from the classroom and the proceedings were consequently entered into with gusto. Whether it is just the memories of youth playing tricks I do not know, but as I look back on the summers we spent in Eisenach I often recall them as being always hot and long. Every so often, however, the days would be interrupted by thunderstorms of such ferocity that I was badly frightened by them, a fear which still remains with me to this very day. We had experienced severe thunderstorms in Kołobrzeg, but they had been positively tame when compared to the brutes unleashed on us in Eisenach. The sky would turn a very dark green, with rolling shapes portending the awesome energy about to be unleashed. Sometimes you would hear the approaching cataclysm before it broke out, but once it arrived, the luminance of the sheet and forked lightning would turn night into day, and the thunder would seem to reverberate around the surrounding hills. The storms which we experienced in Eisenach I still recall with a vividness as if they occurred only yesterday.

One night in November 1938, between midnight and one o'clock in the morning, we were awoken by dreadful heart-rending screams, shouting, breaking glass, and much banging of doors. We rushed to the window. Gangs of Nazis were surrounding nearby houses and dragging the Jewish people out – the old, the young, the sick, the children and the babies. Some were not allowed to dress or even put on shoes as they were raised from their beds and bundled out into the elements. If there were not beaten physically, or abused, their houses were being attacked. I stood at the window to see what was happening, but my mother stormed into the room and shouted: "Get back to bed at once!" She gesticulated at me to get back into bed and pulled me away from the window. She quickly drew the curtains, but I could not understand why I was not allowed to look outside. Seeking enlightenment, I asked, "Has war come to Eisenach?" I thought, indeed I was fairly convinced in my own mind, that this was how war would come to us but my mother replied, "No. This is not a real war. We do not want to become ensnared in what is going on outside, however. You must stay in bed and do not move." I lay there listening to the approaching noise. I was becoming very frightened now and cowered under the covers. Neither Jutta nor I could sleep, and we talked through the night, whilst mayhem and chaos continued unabated all around our cosy home. The crackling of flames and the crash of splintering glass as the windows of neighbouring houses were smashed, the shouting and the screams from both assailants and assaulted, all spoke of events transpiring outside which we two girls found impossible to comprehend. After seemingly coming almost to our front door and us fully expecting that any minute our window would come crashing in about our heads, the noise started to fade away. They, whoever they were, had passed us by, and we had somehow survived unscathed. It was a dreadful experience which left us quite unnerved.

The Synagogue in Eisenach following Kristallnacht

The following day my father went to work as usual and en route, encountered many Jewish shops either burned down or ransacked. All the windows had been smashed and the merchandise pilfered or ruined. When he approached his own shop he was fully expecting the worst, and was astounded when he found it untouched. A day or so later he was told that the gangs were just about to wreck his shop when someone had run up and said that it was owned by an "Aryan." This was not untrue, but again we had been lucky.

I remember seeing the tailor's shop with its windows smashed and seeing the sewing machines through the broken glass and a haberdashers with all the beautiful silks and other materials lying everywhere.

When my mother saw the mess that the SA and Hitler Youth between them were making of the community, she was very upset and wondered what we should do to safeguard our future, given her secret. It would have been naïve to imagine that we were living on other than borrowed time.

It was soon after our arrival in Eisenach that I made friends with Edith Seidel and she quickly became my best friend – even today we keep in close contact. We were in the same class at school and also spent long periods of time together when school was out. We had many good times together enjoying each other's company and confidences, and when war eventually broke out, it strengthened that bond between us. During 1939, the pair of us passed our entrance examinations to join the Eisenach Girls High School, where Jutta and I had been enrolled on our arrival in the town some 18 months earlier. It was a happy time for us all, but Edith and I were especially proud to have gained a place at this school which was so widely renowned for its excellence. We were to take up our studies there in the autumn of 1939.

It was about this time that the little town became swamped with members of the Sturmabteilungen (SA) – the "brownshirts" and Schutzstaffeln (SS). I cannot say that one day they just marched in, but Edith and I suddenly became very conscious that we could not walk around the town without coming across them everywhere. Not long after their arrival, the Hitler Youth movement also came to the fore in this region, and the boys and girls began parading around in the uniform colours of mustard and black. Organisations and clubs were formed to promote the new ideology, and everybody from 10 to 18 years of age had to wear the uniform and attend 'training' sessions. These were held every Wednesday, sometimes in the morning but more often in the afternoon. The group would then march through the streets singing Nazi songs. Each leader walked with pride at the head of his group, carrying the German flag aloft and trying to outdo any other group. The passers-by would look on with smiles, and a certain degree of admiration at the scene. Just as had been the reaction in Kołobrzeg a year or so previously, nobody saw any harm in these general activities, or in the wearing of the uniform – but then they had not yet observed the nastier side of the movement which we had started to experience in Kołobrzeg. It all seemed so innocent to the men and women in the street; and not knowing much about these organisations, Edith, my sister Jutta and I were thrilled to bits with our uniforms, remarking on how smart they looked. We joined in all the activities as enthusiastically as the rest. We belonged. We were accepted. It was a great feeling, but this didn't last long.

Then, one evening, at approximately 7 o'clock I believe, as the family gathered for a light meal, aspirations for the future were shattered as sirens howled across the town like wailing banshees, each one taking up the call and building on it's neighbour until the sound penetrated every corner even into the deepest cellars. The weird sound was not unfamiliar to us and, as we all looked silently at each other, we all knew what it meant. War had broken out. It was the 3rd September 1939.

People all over the world crowded around their wireless sets and listened intently to the news being broadcast. In the early hours of the 1st September, German tanks had crossed into Poland in the first demonstration of Blitzkrieg. Blitzkrieg, lighting war, stunned the targeted nations. Firstly, German bombers would destroy the defender's air power on the ground, and then German panzer divisions of tanks, mechanised infantry and motorised artillery would surge penetratingly into the slower moving defensive armies. This strategy was to be employed against Denmark and Norway in April 1940; the Netherlands, Belgium and Luxembourg in May 1940, and France in May and June 1940.

On 3rd September 1939, France and Britain declared war on the German Reich after Hitler refused to stop the attack against Poland, and those two countries' embassies in Warsaw were surrounded by cheering Poles certain that their country would thereby be saved. Within days that hope had been snuffed out as the Polish defensive strategy broke up under the onslaught from the German forces. The dive-bombers of the Luftwaffe ranged freely over the Polish landscape pouncing on trains loaded with refugees and on columns of retreating troops with their horse-drawn guns and carts. Poland was no match for the mechanised might of the German forces and succumbed to the onslaught, all resistance effectively being neutralised within 5 weeks. Furthermore, the war was escalating dramatically and we were embarked inexorably upon a confrontation which in Europe was to see some 50 million men, women and children perish before it was over. While the roots of this conflict lay in the Great War of 1914-18 which had left the German nation embittered and open to impassioned appeals to national hubris, Nazi goals such as Lebensraum, living space for the German nation, had been used effectively and efficiently by Hitler to fan diplomatic aggression in the face of appeasement policies adopted by Britain and France. Furthermore, Hitler's rearmament drive had left him with a mighty military machine which he had to unleash.

Chapter 3
The Early Days of the War

In Eisenach, life went on very much as normal, except that sirens had been introduced and, so that everyone would know what they sounded like, air-raid alerts were practised on a daily basis. Precautions were introduced to limit the effects of an attack by aircraft and the people were instructed in the actions they should follow on hearing the sirens. One day while my mother was at the shops, the sirens started up, and I hurried down to our cellar. Suddenly there was a lot of banging at the front door and screaming from some SA men outside. If you forgot to put up the blackout you were considered to be a spy and were taken away. On this occasion I had forgotten all about the blackout and a light had been spilling out onto the street. This was a crime I could not escape, but thankfully my mother arrived back just in time and made some excuses about my age and how she would ensure my misdemeanour was never repeated. We suffered a severe warning amid threats of what they would do if the felony was repeated, and I heaved a hearty sigh of relief as they marched off into the darkness. I had been shaking with terror during their tirade, and I burst into tears as my mother drew me towards her.

There were no air-raids around Christmas 1939, and we were able to celebrate a truly peaceful Christmas with some of our friends and relatives. My father's brother, who was a pharmacist in Wittenberg, near Berlin, joined us with his family and we had a magical musical Christmas. My father always played the piano at Christmas and my mother would sing, but for this particular Holy holiday my aunt joined in with them on her violin. It was very festive, especially with the huge Christmas tree which we had bought fresh the previous day. Our maid had helped with all the decorations, and because the ceilings were so high I have recollections of her balancing on the top step of a ladder which was essential to even remotely get her near the uppermost branches. It was a time for jollity and laughter.

On Christmas Eve the candles were lit and the presents would be piled up under the tree and on a nearby table. For my sister and me it was a time of great excitement and anticipation. When everything was ready, my mother would ring a little bell which would summon us into the room. It was then customary to sing a song and to recite a poem before we were allowed to open our presents, but throughout the preface Jutta and I would be stealing glances around the room. We were never showered with gifts, but with the few we always received we were extremely happy. I have never forgotten the doll which was sitting under the tree that Christmas. It was made of pot and its eyes could open and close. Also, if you bent it forward, it would say "Mama". The doll had no hair as such, but had black paint to suggest hair. It was the finest doll I could imagine but, in terms of today's advances in standards of toy production, it was very utilitarian. Among other things we received were a jumper, socks, books, and of course, marzipan which has always been very popular in Germany.

I have known other Christmases when we have perhaps received a new pair of roller skates or ice-skates, and once the biggest surprise of all, a pair of skis: and yet Christmas of 1939 holds memories which had nothing to do with the presents we received. It was the time we gathered strength through the comradeship and compassion of family and friends in the face of an increasingly hostile world. My sister and I were brought up in a privileged society and never knew the hardships and deprivations which accompany poverty and ill-health. We were never short of anything, even when the hard times first started and it became difficult to obtain food and clothing. My mother was not a very good practical housewife, having always had the services of maids to perform the household chores for her, but she was a competent manager and was able to economise when the need demanded. She set about preserving fruit and vegetables, and even made wine out of potatoes. She learnt to exchange certain items like tea, coffee, sweets and sugar for dairy products like butter, and eggs.

The winter of 1939 was very cold and we had to put blankets along the bottom of the window sashes, and put blinds up to the windows to keep the draughts out in addition to the curtains and shutters which had to be closed at night to ensure that no light shone into the street. Our family was well clothed, but we noticed that there were many children who walked to school without either socks or shoes, and of those who did wear shoes, a high proportion had no socks. Poverty was rising in those days and the situation was rapidly deteriorating. One day when my mother was accompanying me to school we noticed a little boy crying in pain from the cold. He wore only a very thin jacket, a white shirt, short trousers and had bare feet. On the very next day my mother brought him some socks and shoes, and the sheer delight on his face was a pleasure to behold. From that very simple beginning she started to collect more and more clothes together, whether they would be our cast-offs or those of our wealthy neighbours, and she would then see that they reached needy children. She did not like to see all the suffering around her and attempted to relieve their distress in whatever ways she could.

In 1940, recognising the deprivations to which its population was bring driven, the Nazi's organised the "Winterhilfswerk" which involved the collection of clothes for those in need. This was a job which was assigned to the Hitler Youth – and a very successful exercise it turned out to be. However, it did highlight that there were insufficient resources for everyone and so it was decreed that all children of Nazi families should have priority of everything. They received free milk at school, if they failed to pass the examinations for High School a place was arranged for them via other channels, and they were allowed the first choice of everything, by right. Furthermore, an "Aryan" mother was expected to produce as least seven children, to strengthen and secure the ascendancy of the pure German stock. Even so, as the Nazis tightened their hold over the German nation, their repression of the Jewish community in South Germany had still not reached the depths to which it had sunk in

Kołobrzeg just before we left. We were still in the clear, and our secret undisclosed, even to Jutta and me. But for how long?

1941 arrived and with it came intense shortages of beer, wine and tobacco. My father was a very heavy smoker and whenever he had to forgo his daily quota of cigars, he would invariably sink into a very bad mood. Potatoes and vegetables were also becoming difficult to obtain, and the meat rations were reduced. The increasing scarcity of more and more commodities led to a thriving black market throughout the German nation and if you had something of value which could be bartered then you were lucky and could survive with comparative ease but there were very many people who were far less fortunate. Crisis conditions were developing.

To ensure that there were more provisions for the pure bred "Aryan" stock, officials of the NSDAP (Nationalsozialistische Deutsche Arbeiterpartei or "Nazi Party") gave instructions that no ration cards were to be issued to full Jews or half Jews, or indeed to "Aryan" husbands or wives who had not divorced their Jewish spouses. Jews were to receive special ration cards from a Jewish agency, and those cards were stamped "Jude" in a colour standing out from the grey background. Those cards were to become of increasing significance, and from October 1942, were the means by which basic food items such as bread, milk, eggs and meat were withheld from their holders.

My parents were becoming more and more worried by the worsening events, but their identity and Jewish connection had yet to be discovered. The fear that their secret would become revealed however, hung over them like a bad dream which would not be dispelled. On 1st September 1941, a new law was passed requiring that every Jew who had reached the age of six years must wear a "star" of yellow material, inscribed with the word "JEW". This label was to be worn on the left side of the coat or dress. It was one evening soon after this statute was enacted, that my parents decided it was time for them to talk with Jutta and me. They told us that they had a very serious matter which they wished to discuss with us, and it would not have been easy for them to puncture our childhood innocence. They explained to us in great detail everything that was happening inside Germany as they saw it, and then finally told us that we were of Jewish descent.

My mother was Jewish! My sister and I were numb with shock at this disclosure. We are Jews. It was a frightening revelation given what we had heard and seen for ourselves. We started to ponder over the possible implications for us personally, but almost at a naively superficial level. What would the children at school say? The previous April I had passed my examinations to the next higher class at my local Girls' High School with flying colours: I'd been so proud of my results and had been looking forward with eager anticipation to the new school year. I earnestly wanted to further my schooling and to make my own mark in life, but with this latest news I could see my aspirations all blowing away in the wind. My lovely secure world was suddenly left in tatters.

One of my friends told me that they were Jewish and that their family was leaving Germany to start afresh in America. Officials of the Nazi Party were permitting Jews to depart but only in the clothes which they were wearing at the time and with no more than 300 Deutschmarks in their pockets. Everything else had to be left behind. Such decisions were very hard for families to reach, but if one truly valued one's life then I suppose such drastic measures had to be faced as necessary evils. The trouble was that the information was hard to come by and when it was, it was often disbelieved as being scaremongering propaganda. My parents were against emigrating and at that time our secret had not been discovered. My best friend Edith, and I, discussed the plight of the Jewish people in general terms but although I could trust her I never told her about us, because I had promised my parents that I would not breathe a word to a living soul. The whole family were carrying on in the fervent hope that the authorities would remain ignorant of our Jewish connection. Up until that time, we had been accepted as normal unassuming folk going about their own business, and there was no suggestion that we might be embroiled in this dreadful debacle.

Then one morning in late 1941, my father received a letter from an official of the NSDAP, summoning him to an urgent meeting which was of crucial importance to him and had direct relevance to his personal safety. He was ushered into a cold, austere room with stone walls and floor, unadorned apart from a picture of Hitler and a German flag, a large wooden table and three unpadded chairs. Facing him across the table as he entered were seated two elderly gentlemen and he was ushered by hand gesture to a chair facing them across the table. They did not introduce themselves but started speaking to him in a very polite manner. Somehow, although they did not explain how, the NSDAP had learned that he was married to a Jewish woman, and he was advised that if he did not divorce her, post haste, his life would be in danger. It came as a bombshell to him, but he just could not imagine how they could possibly believe that he would even contemplate breaking up his very happy and loving marriage. They gave him time to think about their proposition, but his answer was forthright and very much to the point: "Whatever the consequences I will never divorce my wife". The die was cast. Our skeleton was out of the closet. It was the beginning of a very fearful time for the whole family, where every shadow and every knock at our door was viewed with alarm. Our flight from Kołobrzeg to Eisenach would seem to have merely delayed the inevitable.

The very next day the workers and assistants in my father's shop packed up their bits and pieces and left, as did our maid. The NSDAP had forbidden us to engage any staff and it was with mixed feelings that we said our farewells to people who we considered more as close friends than as employees. Their departure however, put a lot of extra work onto my parents who strived to keep the business going against all the odds and to be good parents to us two girls. The effort was a strain which began to show in their faces and in the long hours they kept. As I lay in my bed, I recall often hearing them busily occupying their time and working into the wee small hours.

Christmas 1941 was a very subdued affair compared with previous years. We tried to make the best we could of a bad job, and one or two local friends and acquaintances visited us and we made return visits to them; but the festivities were but a shadow of their former selves. There seemed little about which to rejoice, with food and warmth in short supply. Travel was severely restricted and my father's brother from Wittenberg was unable to bring his family that year. Although we didn't know it then, we had seen him and his family for the last time. He was a member of the SA and was devoted to the cause. He obviously knew of my family's Jewish connection and, on duty one day in 1942, he casually mentioned to his colleagues his tenuous links with a Jew, i.e. his sister-in-law. Without more ado, he was grabbed by his wrists and ankles, and hurled from an upper window of the tall building in which they happened to be at the time. He did not survive the fall. A tearful letter from his widow brought us the sad tidings and we then heard no more from her or her family. My father sank even further into the depths of despair for several weeks following news of his brother's violent death.

Another act of repression which was introduced, was directed against the Catholic Church in Germany, and it was Goebbels who suggested that the priests should be the focal point through whom the Nazis could concentrate their campaign. Thereafter, when a priest said mass, his sermon had to extol the virtues of Hitler and praise the Nazi party. If it didn't, then that priest would be forbidden to hold any future masses – there seemed to be plenty of people willing to spy on such proceedings and report back to the authorities. It was further decreed that religion could no longer be taught in the schools, and some Church bells had to be taken down and silenced. English words were dropped from usage, and it was not permissible to play American phonograph records.

As the civilian population suffered more and more, however, they were buoyed up by stirring reports of how the armies of the glorious Third Reich were advancing on all fronts, and victory would soon be theirs. In 1940, France had fallen, and while the Luftwaffe's relentless attacks had failed to destroy the Royal Air Force during the Battle of

Britain between July and October 1940, the news from all other fronts conveyed to the Fatherland was one of the victorious success upon victorious success. The German armies had invaded the Soviet Union on 22nd June 1941 in Operation Barbarossa, history's largest attack involving three million troops along a 1,800 mile front, and even then were laying siege to Leningrad; in Africa, under General Erwin Rommel, the Deutsches Afrika Korps were sweeping all before them; Rostov, gateway to the oilfields of the Caucasus had been captured on the 20th November 1942; and in the Far East, Germany's allies, the Japanese, under their Commander in Chief, Admiral Isoroku Yamamoto, had launched a devastating attack on the sun-drenched morning of the 7th December 1941 against the American fleet at Pearl Harbour.

Nobody doubted that the superior German forces would push everything before them and they, with their allies Italy and Japan, with whom they signed the Tripartite Pact on 27th September 1940, would emerge supreme. During 1942, significant numbers of foreign workers were very much in evidence on the streets of Eisenach. French and Russian prisoners of war, and workers from Belgium, Holland and Denmark, were pouring into the Third Reich. In the early hours of the morning before dawn broke, we would regularly hear the sound of hard clogs clomping up the road and the clatter of dustbins as the disconsolate foreigners searched for whatever food they could scavenge, even if it were only the scraps thrown out in others' garbage. It reached the stage where my mother started to leave food out by the dustbins for them so sorry was she for their plight, but this had to be undertaken very surreptitiously because we would have been punished for such collaboration, had it been known.

I recall particularly, one Russian man who arrived at our shop with his little son in tow. Both of them looked frozen stiff, with no warm clothes, and we felt very sorry for them both. The man stubbornly refused to take anything without working for us in return; and so, while he chopped wood behind the shop his son sat in our warm kitchen and ate soup. What struck me forcibly was how very polite and well-mannered the boy was. We were unable to learn where his mother might be, and after they had returned on three consecutive days to repeat the identical scenario, they suddenly stopped coming and we saw them no more. We offered up a prayer for their safety and hoped that they survived. Everyone had to be very careful that they were not seen even talking to these foreigners for fear of reprisals, and what these poor unfortunates did when they were not on the streets or during the night-times, we had no idea. The only ones we ever saw were male and we could not but wonder at the agony they must have experienced in being separated from their families, and forced to come so far from their homelands. The German women were starved of male companionship and in some instances, with their men-folk fighting on distant soil, befriended these foreigners. If they became too involved, however, trouble invariably resulted.

One Saturday afternoon I made a surprise visit to my friend Edith's house, where her father told me that she had gone out but there appeared to be some excitement in the market-place. If I had known what was happening I would never have gone near the place, because the episode is now etched indelibly in my memory. However, with Edith unavailable, I was at something of a loose end. It was a beautiful summer's day with the sun high in the clear blue sky. People were all smiles, happy and joyous as they strolled around in their best clothes. Of course, any woman feels better when she can get dressed up in her finery and stroll out under the bright sun. I think most of Eisenach was making the most of a glorious day. The schools were on holiday, which lasted about 7 weeks as I recall, and just before we broke up, Edith and I had received our examination results. I was delighted that they were up to standard and consequently we were both to be transferred into the next class after the holidays. My father had to pay for Jutta and my schooling and always took great interest in our progress ensuring particularly that we never failed to do our homework. The fees for the school were rather expensive but this last term I had done especially well and my parents were exceedingly pleased with my efforts. Because of this, I was enjoying my holiday twice as much as usual.

I was so happy with life and skipped half the way to the market-place wondering what might be the big attraction. From a distance I could see that a large crowd of people were milling around, shouting, laughing, etc. – there was such a commotion that I just had to see what was happening. I was small and could ascertain nothing from the back, but the people were so closely packed that I could not push my way through either. I asked somebody why it was so busy and a stout lady standing nearby, looked down as me with such a gaze which I can only describe as amazement. She slowly took off her glasses, and then said: "Come, I'll show you what is going on". She pushed her way through the crowd hauling me along in the clear vortex left immediately behind in the generous wake. We arrived at the front and she moved to one side so that I could see. Fear welled up inside me. I couldn't get away from the crowd pressed against me from the rear. I could only look and absorb the scene before me.

Two poles had been stuck into the ground. To one was tied a man with his hands bound tightly behind him, and to the other was a woman similarly restrained. Their hair had been completely shorn, and it was obvious that this spectacle was arranged by the Nazis to discourage fraternisation. Underneath the lady's feet was a placard which read "I am a German woman and have associated with a Pole"; the verse under the man's feet was in similar vein. Somebody said in a loud voice that we were allowed to walk round these people, to look at what happened to all those who associated with foreigners, to spit upon them, and to throw anything we liked at them. The crowd surged forward behind me and I was pushed towards the lady first until I was looking up into her face. She looked down at me with such very sad eyes. They were full of terror, and tears were running down her tortured face. I can still remember that look she gave me to this very day. She did not intend to frighten or intimidate me, I am sure, but somehow she looked right into the depths of my soul. I looked back at her and offered up a silent prayer as I was pushed onwards and past her. She was beyond help and caught up in the Nazi propaganda machine. I had to drag myself away from both of them as the crowd pressed in, crying for blood. Somebody behind me shouted that the best was yet to come. I should have fled from the square, but no! I waited and hoped that they would be released after the torment and trauma to which they had already been subjected.

They were untied from the poles, roughly manhandled over to a large lorry and secured by long ropes to the rear bar. The lorry moved off very slowly and the two captives trotted behind it. Remorselessly the throttle was wound up until the two were running as fast as they could to keep the pace. The people were sneering, throwing stones, and generally ridiculing them. The woman was first to collapse, and as she fell she brought the man down too. The lorry didn't stop however, and they were dragged round and round the market place, with the crowd still baying after them. I could look no more and averted my eyes, staring down at the ground – but I could hear their screams as their flesh was being torn from their bodies. Blood streaked and mottled the cobbles of the square. Suddenly I was aware that everything had gone silent. The lorry had departed and the people were starting to disperse, I would like to think, very sheepishly. The rowdiness had all gone, probably as the enormity of what they had just witnessed sunk in. Nobody was able to find out what happened to the hapless victims after that; but as a child, the incident upset me more than I could possibly have imagined and left a lasting impression that was to haunt me and cause me sleepless nights for weeks to come.

I went slowly home, the earlier gaiety and fun totally wrung from me. I pondered on what could turn my fellow citizens into a lynch mob baying for blood. People who I might see time and time again going about their normal business, had suddenly been stirred up into a hate-filled senseless crowd. I blurted out to my parents what I had just witnessed and how dreadful it had made me feel. They were very annoyed and admonished me for going to the market place. They also pointed out how essential it was that we maintained a low profile, and that I should keep away from any gatherings which might occur in the future. I could not sleep that night, tormented by those sad and fearful eyes, which still haunt me to this day.

Jutta and I spent our holidays in a number of ways. We would help our mother with household chores, such as cleaning and washing, running errands, or preparing the fruit and vegetables which she would later preserve. On other days we would play tennis with Edith, or swim in one of the lakes. Edith lived fairly close to us and therefore we were able to spend a lot of time together. Eisenach also boasted a small roller-skating rink and I went there frequently to practise for a grand opening ceremony to be held at a much larger rink which had been constructed recently in Erfurt. I was one of those chose to perform there and had to collect special wooden roller-skates from a nearby castle where a number of high ranking and titled Nazis lived.

There was no lift, of course, and the stairs seemed endless until we reached the top. We looked at each other and giggled, like teenagers do. I knocked at a huge oak door. A voice begged us to come in. Two SS men sat at a big polished desk surrounded by large paintings of Hitler, Goering, Himmler and other important leaders. "Heil Hitler! little girls" they said. "We understand that you have come to collect your skates?" They were very nice and polite. They introduced themselves, and the taller and more handsome man was Adolf Eichman! They talked to us for a while and wished us luck in our event. With our skates, walking back with happiness, we couldn't wait to tell our parents the whole story. We felt very proud to have been given the chance to meet these important men. Sadly, I learned later that Eichman was in reality an evil man who achieved world-wide notoriety later for his involvement in the extermination camps.

It was important to take part in all the activities because it helped to relieve any suspicions that you might not wholly support the Nazi movement. Roller-skating, swimming, cultural trips, etc. were all organised by the Nazis for the youth of the country, and Jutta, Edith and I joined with fervent enthusiasm. I thoroughly enjoyed most of the promotional activities anyway and did not find my participation a chore. I was not so enthused by the indoctrination and propaganda in the classroom. We had to write essays praising and applauding the things the Nazis were doing for the populace – I recall one in particular which was about 'letting the wheels turn for victory' and my effort was chosen to be read out in front of the whole class. Luckily it was for praise, but when you are accorded such preferential treatment and called to the front of the class, you could never be sure if it was for praise, or for ridicule to be heaped upon you by the teacher and your classmates.

Me and my rollerskates

Anyway, I had been selected to travel with a small group of girls to Erfurt where we were housed for a week in a hostel under the supervision of the matronly lady. She was a sort of mother figure to us looking to our needs and accompanying us on our daily excursions to the rink where we would practise our roller-skating routine and familiarise ourselves with the venue. Then, on the final day, we took part in the competition proper. This was designed primarily to glorify the Nazi Party and demonstrate what an excellent job it was doing for the youth of the country. Everywhere uniformed officers and men stood or strutted, and there was much excitement amongst the competitors and the audience. There was colour and spectacle aplenty, to take everyone's mind off the war and allow them to escape temporarily the everydayness of their existence. I felt really proud to be participating in such a prestigious event and my parents came from Eisenach to watch me on this momentous day. My knees were knocking with nervousness as my friends and I took to the floor and, while we produced a very passable and presentable performance, we won nothing. To have taken part was more than enough for me. The rink was immense and, as we left after the customary speeches, I wished that we would have had such a magnificent arena in Eisenach. At least I consoled myself with the thought that in the future I would be able to use the Erfurt facility whenever I chose because it was not too far from our home town. Unfortunately, the following year the whole arena was flattened by bombs and my excursions to the rink had to cease.

Autumn arrived with a vengeance in 1942. Suddenly the cold weather was with us, and the winds whipped the colourful leaves from the trees. The badgers and foxes disappeared earlier than usual and the birds migrated to the warmer climes. In our forest there were many chestnut trees and in autumn there were plentiful supplies of their fruit to collect. During the week's half-term holiday from school we used to go to the forest, pick the chestnuts, and sell them to a local farm. A lot of children enjoyed doing this and there was a genuine rivalry between us to see who could gather the most. The more adventurous would climb the trees, making a game out of the whole proceedings, while others pinched the chestnuts from those who had made the effort of collecting them. Time hung heavily for the children, who had to make their own amusements.

Also on the outskirts of Eisenach was a large pond and in the winter it would regularly freeze over. Often were there happy hours

Jutta and I, with many children far and wide, would spend ice-skating there. Our parents had bought us proper skates for this purpose but many of the other children were not so fortunate. In our enthusiasm, we sometimes went onto the ice when it was not sufficiently thick and one day Jutta was skating out on the ice with some other children when it gave way under them and she plunged into the water. To this day I do not recall exactly how she and the others got out, because pandemonium ensued. The ice cracked further as those in the water tried to pull themselves out or their friends on the bank ventured onto the ice to try and rescue them. The vast majority of us finished up sodden and frozen to the marrow as the water and the biting wind cut through our clothing. Nobody died but as we all hurried back to the warmth and comfort of our homes, I think we all reflected on a well-learnt lesson.

Edith had two brothers, Hermann and Rolf, who were called up to serve their country in the armed forces. Hermann, the elder brother, was sent to the Russian front and every time he returned home on leave he brought back gruesome stories of the savagery and inhumanity being meted out.

"It's an absolute disgrace to the German army, the way our troops are being ordered to treat the Russian women and children, who are no more combatants than you, Edith, or Anneliese there. And yet they are shown no mercy, and the more we assault them the happier our officers seem. They are attacked, physically abused, sometimes raped and dragged screaming from their homes which are then set ablaze. We are then ordered to march on to the next hamlet or village to repeat the same treatment to their inhabitants. The poor ravaged people are then left in the bitter cold, defenceless against temperatures which drop down to 20 degrees below freezing. In such conditions they usually freeze to death before starvation claims them. I feel so helpless. On my own though, there is nothing I can do to help them or prevent the atrocities."

Hermann always arrived home unexpectedly and thus his arrival could never be anticipated by his family. Such homecomings were a cause for much celebrating however, as were those when his brother returned, and I was usually invited to join in with his family and friends. Rarely did the two brothers' visits coincide but I looked forward to those gatherings as high spots in my fairly full calendar. On one occasion the return was not the happy event to which he had become accustomed.

It was just days before Christmas 1942 when a young and happy Hermann made his way joyously back to his parent's house in Eisenach. It was a glorious winter's day with the brilliant sun successfully holding a frost at bay and, despite the heavy bag he had slung over his shoulder, he decided to walk all the way from the station. He strolled the familiar territory as fast as he could, a cheery bounce in his step, eager to be home after months of separation from his loved ones. It wasn't often one had leave over Christmas and it was an extra reason for celebration. He thought of the surprise it would be for his family at having him home for the festivities, and his step quickened at the mere thought of it. From a distance he was able to pick out the hotel in which his parents resided and which they had run as a successful business until the outbreak of hostilities had decimated trade. He crossed the road, whistling gaily, not a care in the world, and stood before the huge oak door which was always open during the hours of daylight. He closed the door quietly behind him and walked up the few steps leading to the restaurant area on the right hand side of the entrance hall. "Hallo. I'm home. Where is everybody?" This was very unusual. Normally the restaurant was busy at lunchtimes serving meals and drinks, but today there wasn't anyone sitting at the small bar and there were only a couple of tables occupied by patrons. Laughing and shouting he dashed across the hallway into the private quarters off to the left of the entrance but nobody was there. He continued on down the corridor to the bowling alley at the far end. "Hallo. Your elder son is home. Stop playing games." There were a few men in the alley playing and generally enjoying themselves, but his intrusion hardly evoked more than a sideways glance so engrossed were they in what they were doing. This was getting ridiculous. He hurried through to the fine garden at the back of the house where meals were served during the summer and where on fine afternoons homemade cakes were regularly provided on the lawns, together with delicious coffee or tea. There was nobody out there. Well, they had to be somewhere. They wouldn't leave the hotel to run itself unattended.

Hermann ran back into the hotel and took the stairs two at a time, calling out and shouting all the while. He tried several doors but the rooms were empty.

"Where are you all? Has everyone gone to bed? Come on you lazybones. Stop playing around," yelled a somewhat exasperated Hermann by this time. Where was everybody? His father suddenly slipped quietly out of one of the rooms along the corridor in front of him and held up his hand in a resigned attempt to silence him. "Hermann. What a surprise," he whispered haltingly.

"Come in here my son. I am afraid I have some bad news for you. It's not how I would have liked to welcome you home but I am sorry to have to tell you that your mother has just passed away."

His father was sobbing as he led Hermann into the room where his mother lay surrounded by some of her friends including Edith, all with tears in our eyes. Hermann stood there transfixed, not able to comprehend the reality of the situation suddenly confronting him. He apologised for making so much noise and sunk morosely into his own thoughts. It was my first experience of death at first hand as it were, and I like to think that she went peacefully and in the bosom of her family where she was so loved. Edith's mother had always taken great pleasure from strolling in her garden and admiring the flowers when they were out or the wild life that abounded there. On this particular day, the sunshine had encouraged her to take a turn around the garden in spite of the cold. One of the hotel guests had also been taking the air at the time and had rushed to her when she suddenly collapsed. She was carried inside and taken upstairs to her bed where she died a little later.

Edith was the most openly upset and took her mother's death very badly. She frequently visited us thereafter and seemed to cling to my mother for support and guidance, to such an extent that she became more like one of our family. Edith's parents owned a large grand piano which she had started to play when she was only six years old. She was very talented and was able to play classical music and jazz with equal competence. Often my father would play duets with her and I would admire the beautiful melodies that would flow from their nimble fingers. Some 18 months after her mother's death, Edith's aunt who also lived in the hotel, married Edith's father and they continued to run the hotel together. Edith was the youngest and the favourite in the Seidel family, but in the summer following her mother's death she had to give up her schooling in order to help in the hotel where her hard work and application was essential for its survival as a growing concern, so difficult was it to find trustworthy hired-help. Her great loss and the upheaval in her domestic life which resulted from it, brought her and me closer together than we had ever been before.

The Nazis seemed to have forgotten about us, and for over a year now had not bothered our family at all. My father had heard nothing since telling the NSDAP of his decision to remain with my mother; although from that decisive moment back in 1941, his business had suffered as he tried to run it, occasionally single-handedly, but generally with my mother's assistance. This had put a lot of pressure onto my mother, who also had to cope with all the household chores herself too. My sister and I helped out as much as we could, but we were young and had our schooling to consider. Indeed, it was rare for my sister to help because of the important school work she had to undertake at home and, in my view, this aversion she had to getting her hands dirty. I considered that she was merely skiving, but her objections seemed to satisfy our mother. The hardest work and the task which I disliked the most, was undoubtedly the washing and although we had a wash-house, everything had to be boiled up in a large tub. The whole washing procedure could take a full day even in the summer when drying conditions were much better. In the winter, the only place in which we could dry clothes was up in the attic and invariably they never dried there due to the severity of the winters, the lack of any form of heating, and the inadequacies of the ventilation.

My mother had always had the services of a maid right up until we were required to dismiss all of our employees late in 1941 and, because she had never done any housework herself before, this was a particularly gruelling period for her. I felt very sorry for her as I watched her struggling to cope with activities alien to her. It was not just the hard and heavy work which troubled her, or the hours she had to help in the shop to ensure we had enough to sustain us. She was weighed down by the constant fear that the Nazis might decide anytime that we were worthy of their attention. Christmas 1942 came around like so many Christmases before it, and my parents attempted to make it as festive as they could. The atmosphere had changed however, and we could all sense that this year it was somehow different. Edith's loss the previous week still hung heavily upon us but the news on the wireless was also far more depressing. It was the first Christmas I had known where there were only the four of us to celebrate it, and particularly, our thoughts turned to my father's brother's absence and his family's tragedy. My parents tried their best to hide their grave concern for the future and gave us a Christmas we could look back on with fond and pleasant memories. Our hearts were not especially uplifted however as 1943 slipped quietly in through the back door.

Our home was a detached villa on the outskirts of Eisenach, reached up an unmade, tree-lined road which rose steeply from the town and then wound its way past our house and on into the country. The dwelling comprised three storeys with a cellar beneath, and a large rear garden. The front door gave onto a dark hall, off which led doors to the dining room, a study for father, mother's room, and a large kitchen. A staircase rose from the hall to two large bedrooms and a boxroom in which a sewing lady who used to come regularly, would sit and mend sheets, etc. There was a further flight of stairs giving access to a large attic room which had been occupied by the maid until she was forced to leave. I had always wanted that room for my own, and that Christmas of 1942 I got my wish. Unknown to my sister or me, my parents had completely refurbished the attic and had thoroughly cleaned the floor and walls. Thus, for the first time in my life, I did not have to share a bedroom with my sister. I was 13 years old.

In the first couple of years of the war, there had been very few air raids over Eisenach during the night, and our slumbers had passed largely undisturbed. There had been occasional sorties during the day however, and there was a very significant upturn in the number of such day raids soon after the Americans entered the conflict at the end of 1941. There was some puzzlement over the intended targets of these attacks however. Eisenach had a BMW factory, later to become the present-day Auto-Werk-Eisenach, another car factory to the North of the town, a brewery, and a spinning mill in Katarien Street. In our view, none of these had particular strategic importance, and as far as we could see none were seriously damaged throughout the duration of the war. The bombers seemed to us to concentrate their attention more on the residential areas of town, and we could only surmise that they were after the many senior Nazis who lived there.

In Germany, the air-raid shelters were located in the cellars under the houses, and periodically these were inspected to check that they were still safe to use. Initially, when the frequency of the raids increased, my family spent many nights in our cellar but, as the seemingly unrelenting bombing campaign continued unabated, my father became more and more concerned at the adequacies, or perhaps I should say inadequacies, of our perfunctory protection. Our confidence in the ability of our refuge to withstand the furious onslaught from the heavens was rapidly diminishing, and the idea of being buried in the cellar did not appeal. In one bombing raid, several of our neighbours were buried alive when their houses collapsed upon them. Many others did not have cellars in which they could seek refuge, and since the authorities were slow in providing alternative shelter, many died. Schmelzer Street was one area which suffered appalling casualties because of the lack of adequate protection.

During the daytime air raids, I felt no safer. Our school had no bunker and we had to stay in the classroom and continue with our lessons. As you sat in the class and listened to the drone of the aircraft overhead and the crumps from exploding bombs, it was hard to concentrate on what the teacher was saying. Indeed the teacher probably had one ear cocked to the sounds outside and every so often we would be told to crouch down under our desks when the noise seemed to be especially close. We were all terrified.

There was considerable relief therefore, when a huge bunker was built near our villa to afford shelter for the many hundreds of people living in the immediate vicinity. We took advantage of this reinforced concrete sanctuary at the earliest opportunity and regularly spent our nights there. Jews and animals were prohibited from entering its portals, but fortunately nobody knew of my mother's background and we certainly had no intention of appearing not to belong within this utilitarian facility. However, we did not know how long our secret would remain undisclosed, and we were increasingly conscious of the need for care and vigilance.

Following a bomb blast close to the communal shelter, my parents decided that it was no longer safe for us to continue using the bunker and instead, on an alert, we would make our way into the surrounding woods. We felt far safer there, although it was not very pleasant being dragged out of bed from a deep sleep in the middle of the night when the sirens sounded, and then having to stumble in near darkness for 20 minutes or so into the woods. We were still expected to attend school the following day, even though we might have had little or no sleep that night. It was not long before such conditions began to take their toll on our systems, and we reached the stage where we were forever tired, irritable and tense. At first, the area of forest in which we chose to sit out the bombing raids was fairly welcoming, as we drew comfort and strength from the rocks into which we snuggled and the canopy of leaves overhead which hid the horrors beyond. Then the bombs started to fall in the woods, amongst the rocks, shattering our haven and illusions of security. We could not understand why the Americans should be bombing the forest, although we were later informed that large numbers of Nazis were fleeing there whenever an air-raid was signalled, rather than attending the official bunkers. There was nowhere else for us to go, and so we continued to seek refuge among the trees because it was probably better than remaining near the town centre.

One evening when we arrived at our customary spot however, we were unable to believe our eyes. Indeed we had to double check that we were in our usual area, because what we saw was totally unrecognisable. The forest had been destroyed. The beautiful trees, the winding paths through green ferns and mosses, even the rocks, were no more. They had vanished in an orgy of devastation and havoc on a grand scale. Only blackened and twisted tree stumps, curling smoke plumes and pulverised rock met our gaze. There was no option but in future to venture even further from the centre of Eisenach, and that meant even less sleep for all of us. For some time afterwards, I had nightmares at the thoughts of what it would have been like if we had been sheltering there in the forest, at the exact moment when the American bombers chose to release their rain of death.

The air-raids at night were mounted generally by the British, while the Americans came by day. The night raids especially, had increased in ferocity of late and we were all getting less sleep. Even after a few sleepless nights, it became almost impossible to attend school and concentrate on the lessons without falling asleep at our desks. Eisenach was not a very strategic target and the Royal Air Force were by now launching their thousand bomber raids on such targets as Essen, Emden, Hamburg, Duisburg, Dusseldorf, and Cologne. The worst night we experienced was when the nearby BMW factory was attacked. It was a dreadfully frightening experience and the ground shook beneath our feet as each payload exploded.

Still, with the arrival of 1943, we sensed that matters were coming to a head and that the next twelve months would see significant changes. Was this to be the year that peace returned to our troubled planet, or would it end in upheaval and sorrow for us? We did not put our feelings into words but we all knew instinctively that things were about to change.

Chapter Four
The Fear Grows

It was in February, on a bitterly cold day, while my parents were serving together in the shop, that two men in civilian clothes walked into the shop. They waited until all the customers had left the premises and then asked my father to go with them. It must have been one of those days when we had a school holiday, because I was in the back of the shop helping, and heard everything that went on. My parents always gave me a little job to keep me busy when I visited the shop, and that day I was unpacking boxes and wrapping goods in quantities ready for sale.

Suddenly I heard a man's voice, "Herr Wegner. You will come along with us. If you come quietly nobody will notice anything untoward. Alternatively, you can resist or create a fuss, but in the end you will still come with us." I rushed over to the slightly ajar door between the shop and my cubby hole, screwing my eye to the crack and hoping that they could not see me. I'd taken an instant dislike to these men and nothing I saw from my hidden vantage point dispelled that. Both men were wearing a hat and a long light-coloured trench coat. They didn't want to buy anything, and had on their faces what appeared to me like triumphant grins competing with sneers of derision. They looked objectionable people and not the sort with whom one should argue.

"Where are you taking me?" enquired my father, a trifle contritely. "My wife ought to know where we are going."

They didn't answer him but started pushing him towards the door. When my mother realised that they had no intention of letting my father get dressed properly, even though it was a bitterly cold day with an icy wind blowing, she ran through to the back of the shop to fetch his warm winter coat, whispering to me to keep quiet and stay where I was as she rushed by me.

On her return to the front shop, she looked very pale and was in a state of shock.

"Please tell me where you are taking my husband," she implored the two men, but as they pushed her aside one replied, "He will not be gone long." The aura of menace surrounding them and the smirks which they exchanged back and forth, discouraged me from dashing to my mother's side. She rushed over to my father and hugged him quickly, their lips meeting fleetingly, before the Gestapo marched him away, one on each side of him. She'd known they were Gestapo men without their saying, and as the shop door closed behind them I rushed to my mother's side and we watched wrapped in each other's arms until my father, Kurt Wegner, had passed from view.

I had to admire my mother at that moment. She never let on as to what had just happened and carried on serving and busying herself around the shop as she would on any normal day. Several customers entered the shop and my mother managed a smile for all of them. Although my mother's thoughts must have been far away, she was able to indulge in a little small-talk, and hide her pounding heart. Only I was aware of the inner turmoil she must have been undergoing and, as I fought to hold back my tears and be strong like her, I stayed quietly at her side, helping her. I was finding it more and more difficult to cope.

Then one bright afternoon after school had finished, an old, kindly-looking gentleman came into the shop where my mother was serving single-handedly, while I was busy in the back. He was not dressed in the Gestapo uniform of hat and standard trenchcoat, but instead wore a brown jacket, green shirt, no tie, and his baggy dark-brown trousers lacked any sign of a crease. He was wearing black unpolished shoes and his cap almost totally hid his hair from view. He had a ruddy complexion and certainly hadn't the intimidating air of the SS or SA. At the same time he didn't act as if he were a customer and we did not recognise him as someone who we had met before. "Frau Wegner," he hesitantly whispered as he leaned across the counter somewhat conspiratorially towards my mother, "You do not know me or of me, but I know all about you and your family. I come as a friend and want to help you. Do not be afraid." They walked to the end of the counter so that it did not stand between them, but I was still able to hear what was being said.

"Firstly I bring you news of your husband, Frau Wegner. He is alive and well; and has been taken to Buchenwald Concentration Camp." Wide-eyed, shocked and trembling, my mother could not find words for a reply. We'd all heard dreadful tales of what transpired in such places, much of it seeming to defy credibility. The thought that my father might be suffering torture and torment in a camp was too hard to contemplate as our imaginations ran riot. Those who knew Eichmann had reported that he personally had witnessed the deaths of Jews in the cruellest of circumstances. Thus, for example, stories had been circulating that at Auschwitz Concentration Camp, he had set up the iron-ring torture. In this, a prisoner was chained to a wall and his hands tied up above his head. His eyes were then bored or plucked out, his ribs crushed by blows from a stave, his throat pierced, and his back kicked in. The prisoner was then left to hang there until pronounced dead. I can well imagine the thoughts coursing through my mother's head on news that my father was in a Concentration Camp. My own thoughts were awash with emotion and I strained to hear more of what they were saying. I think my mother must have decided that I had overheard enough, assuming she knew I was in earshot, because after this devastating news they moved closer together and spoke more quietly. I could hear little of what then transpired.

As their conversation drew to an end and they walked together towards the door, he must have been aware of how distraught and frightened my mother had become during their discussions and he hastened to calm her, asserting that he was doing everything in his power to help. "I have been in contact with the City Doctor, and between us we have hit upon a plan to have Kurt returned to you," he said reassuringly. "We are confident that we will soon have him back with you." The City Doctor was our own doctor so if he was involved we were reasonably confident that he would deliver what he promised. I heard no more however. They talked a long time near the door but I never did find out what it was about, or indeed, who this sympathetic visitor was. I served the few customers who came into the shop while he was still with us to avoid the pair of them being disturbed, but when I glanced over in their direction they would be talking and gesticulating as if they were discussing the wares. My mother kept a lot to herself, I suppose because she was fearful that Jutta or I might say something to other people or to our schoolmates.

We could only surmise what our father might be going through, but obviously something terrible had happened which could have serious consequences for the rest of us. After a couple of weeks had passed, following our new-found friend's visit to the shop, and we had still not received any further information, my mother laid plans with some friends of ours who owned a restaurant. Although they were very pro-Nazi, they were supportive towards her and promised that if she was taken away too, they would look after Jutta and me. One evening, she drew Jutta and me to her and explained to us what we were to do if ever we arrived home and found her not there. She warned us to be prepared for almost any eventuality. It was a bit hard for me to comprehend the true situation and I pondered long and hard the possibility of running away somewhere. Surely, I would be able to find a place where nobody would be able to bother me. Such thoughts were impracticable of course, particularly while my mother was still with us. However, this brief talk with my mother brought home to me, perhaps more so than had my father's forcible removal, how perilous was our position. Fear was with us both day and night from then onwards.

It was not just her concern for our personal well-being that worried my mother. She was also agonising about the future of the shop and our ability to make a living. Once people got to know about us they would boycott our emporium because, by then, it was a shameful and punishable offence to purchase anything from a Jew. Our clientele had fallen off slightly when our staff were required to leave but now, if my father was an "Aryan" and he was in a Concentration Camp, what hope had my mother and we two girls got on our own. The Hitler Youth would surely picket the place and make our future a misery – and yet it did not happen! It was strange, and we could not understand it. People still came into the shop, and business kept up. It was just that my father was not there any more.

The fear and agony remained in spite of everything and it stayed with us throughout each day and night. As my mother toiled daily in the shop she worried that the Gestapo might walk in and spirit her away – particularly as it might be while Jutta and I were out at school; or perhaps Jutta and I would not come home from school one day because the Gestapo had lain in wait for us outside the school, or even worse, stormed into the classroom and torn us away from our class-mates: and every night at home as she performed her household chores she would listen out for any footfall that might stop outside the house in case it was someone arriving to take her away from us. I had very similar worries to those of my mother, but we had to hide our feelings and thoughts from our friends and neighbours. It was imperative that we acted perfectly normally on our way to and from school lest we give ourselves away through our furtive actions. We could trust nobody but ourselves – informers were everywhere.

The Gestapo were still bent upon rooting out all Jews and other "unacceptables", whether they be those who had been overlooked in the initial sweep or those who had been in hiding and subsequently found. Many were given away by Germans who accepted the concept of a "clear and pure race", having been brain-washed by the unrelenting propaganda. This propaganda was everywhere, in the halls, on the hoardings, on the radio, and especially in the schools. Children were probably most susceptible to such attacks and genuinely believed that this regime was both good and worthy of their wholehearted support. Many could see that their fathers were in work again after years of poverty, and for their families things had improved significantly. They knew nothing else, nothing of the evil, and believed the propaganda, taking up the cause with great enthusiasm. Only a very few people knew the real horrors of what was happening in the cause of purification and promotion of the true German identity – and they remained silent. The unfortunates who did not meet the Aryan criterion were dragged out onto the streets by the Nazis and their henchmen, assisted invariably by members of the Hitler Youth. They were then paraded in some sort of pseudo-spectacle designed to demonstrate to the general populace how the evil and corruption in their society was being weeded out and removed. The cleansing process had widespread support and flowed like a mountain stream pushing all the flotsam and dross before it.

Jutta and Anni, 1941

Then it happened. One sunny but cold afternoon we were to experience the dreadful debacle at first hand. A neighbour came running to us, pointing out that more than fifty people had been found that morning and that they were about to be brought through the streets. We didn't want to go out and look, but not to do so would create gossip which in turn could lead to our betrayal. It was a very sad scene which befell our eyes and one which we would have avoided had we not felt compelled to bear witness. There were women with young children, women with babies in arms, pregnant women, and children with no one to whom they could cling and seek comfort. There were a few old men but the group was virtually exclusively female or young. What had happened to the able-bodied men we could but wonder. It was fairly clear that the sorry band of outcasts passing before us had been dragged from their homes in no more than they had on at the time. It was bitterly cold and yet most had no outdoor coats, some had no shoes, and they were a pitiful sight to behold, as they dragged themselves wearily by, rarely looking to either side but keeping their eyes cast down on the ground. Man's inhumanity to his fellow beings would seem to know no boundaries. The fear grew in all our hearts as the bedraggled procession passed by and from our view.[1]

How long would it be before we were hauled out on a similar long trek to apparent oblivion? My mother's nerves became worse, anxiety gnawing at her insides like an insidious cancer. She suffered with more and more headaches as the days of her lonely vigil passed, and she often felt so ill that there were times when she could not open the shop. During this period it was I who had to look after her, to console her, and to try to give her hope to keep going. Jutta seemed either not to be too bothered about her mother, or she was simply trying to deal with her own feelings and fears by shutting herself up inside: insulating herself from the realities around her.

Some three months had passed since my father departed with the two Gestapo men, and still there had been no word from him. Our only news had been from our friendly visitor who had told us of Papa's removal to the Concentration Camp, but even he had not returned after his early promises of hope.

One evening the three of us were sitting together discussing the lessons at school that day. The class I was in had been asked to undertake a project which involved my building an ark, and I had not been making a particularly good job of it. I asked my mother for some help and she introduced a bit of fun into the proceedings. Jutta and I scurried round looking for materials that could be incorporated, matchsticks here, cotton and threads there. We made some glue and

---

1 In September 1941 145 Jews of the town were interned in a house at Goethestraße 48; they were deported in May 1942 to Belzec and Theresienstadt

laughed happily together as the ark rapidly took on shape. It was nearly finished when there was a sudden knock at the door. This was not how we had expected the Gestapo to come for us, and my mother's heart started pounding with fear. She looked at us – we looked at her, and Jutta and I huddled closer together on the sofa. We could even hear her heart pounding as our own sent blood flushing towards our heads, pulsing wildly at our temples. The adrenalin was flowing as never before. My mother could not get up. She sat there as if paralysed.

Then again, another knock came, but this time a lot fainter. Surely, this could not be the Gestapo – we hoped! She got up wearily, with an air of resignation, and slowly made her way to the front door. The lock turned grudgingly in her shaking fingers and she opened the front door. There stood my father! He had come back. Her amazement and joy at seeing him on our front step was too much for her. After what she had imagined awaited her on the doorstep, the floods of relief overwhelmed her and tears streamed down her face.

She could not find words, so overcome was she emotionally at seeing him again. She ushered him before her into the warm room and I don't know what he may have thought as he saw two pairs of eyes woefully looking up from the sofa. Jutta and I had not been sure what to expect to see coming through the doorway but the silence which had followed the opening of the front door had left me somewhat puzzled. When we saw it was Papa walking into the room it took a few moments for that reality to register; but when it had percolated through into our consciousness, we leapt to our feet and threw our arms around him so overjoyed were we to see him back. After the initial euphoria, we each gave him warm and grateful hugs for his safe return. We were all smiles and settled down to receive his news. He looked very, very tired and his face was drawn and pale. His eyes were sunken, he had lost quite a bit of weight, and he was shivering. We had eyes only for him, hardly able to believe that he really was with us again. It was nearly midnight and there was insufficient time for him to tell us what had transpired in those long months we had been separated. Indeed, I don't think he was really up to it. He took some hot food while we three sat around gazing at him scarcely able to believe the evidence of our eyes. As soon as he had finished eating we all retired to bed, but the following evening we gathered around to hear of his experiences at Buchenwald Concentration Camp.

Until then the information we had gleaned was more rumour and speculation than hard facts because few returned to tell their tales. The conditions sounded absolutely appalling, and I'm sure that our father must have spared us some of the more lurid details. For young girls such as Jutta and I, it did not sound at all inviting, and was an experience we should try to avoid at whatever the cost. I never did find out to what torment or humiliation he had been subjected, but the unsavoury episode had certainly left an indelible impact upon him. I guess he told my mother far more than he told us but whatever the true story of his incarceration my father was never again quite the same hearty outgoing fellow that I used to remember. Apparently, we had our doctor to thank for my father's release. It was he who had pointed out to the Authorities that my father was an Aryan and had been unjustly detained. He also averred that my father was really a very sick man. As a direct result of this intervention, Papa had been released from the Camp – but that was not to be the end of the story.

A few days later he received a summons to attend the NSDAP office. My father immediately contacted our doctor for advice and was told by him to drink lots of strong coffee before keeping the appointment. It was believed that palpitations were a sign of a bad heart, and the coffee would give him palpitations. When I arrived home from school that day, I found my father in a dreadful state. He had drunk vast quantities of coffee, which was far too strong for him, and he was suffering badly as a consequence. My mother was at the shop and was unaware of his condition. I tried to calm him and make him rest, but he insisted on setting off for the office even though in any other circumstances he would not have dared venture forth. I watched him struggle off down the road and was worried all the time he was gone – if he collapsed en-route I would never be able to forgive myself.

He later told us that on arrival at the office he was ordered to strip off and then was thoroughly examined by two doctors while a nurse took notes in the background. They asked him many questions. "Why were you released from the Concentration Camp?" one queried loudly as he peered into my father's ears. The other started hitting his chest while listening to his lungs. "You're not really ill, are you?" the other said. They went over him with a fine toothcomb and made comments to each other which my father didn't really understand. They seemed to be paying little regard to his shaking hands and generally poor demeanour. While he was being examined however, my father suddenly slumped to the floor in a faint.

This seemed to be a sufficient answer for the Nazis who had clearly had enough and simply left him lying there. He vaguely remembers them instructing one of their helpers to get rid of him because he was a sick man, and he suddenly found himself ejected onto the street with his clothes thrown out on top of him. People looked across at him as he struggled to dress but no one came to his aid. He literally had to drag himself home although he was feeling so poorly that he found every movement an immense effort. However, he eventually arrived back at our house where he fell into my mother's arms. The three of us had been anxiously awaiting his return and it was great to have him back in the bosom of the family. Thankfully, nobody associated with the Buchenwald Camp bothered him again following that incident.

Shortly after this examination at the NSDAP surgery my father was astonished to be called up for the Eisenach Fire Brigade. We took comfort from the fact that it suggested matters were returning to a semblance of normality and our position had been accepted. We felt that with his call to service, we could breathe more easily once again. A friend of my father's, who was an Italian by birth, was also called upon to join the same Fire Brigade unit, which acted in a sort of Home Guard capacity. This Italian friend, who was also a frequent customer of ours, owned a restaurant at which we regularly dined on Sundays, and my father was really delighted to learn that they would be together in the same unit. It was interesting for us to learn that he had also been medically examined as had my father, and then had heard nothing further until his call-up papers had arrived out of the blue.

Meanwhile my mother continued to conduct the business and run the home single-handedly. She also frequently visited my father who had to live away from home and she reported back to us that he was being treated well. He was very worried at having to leave my mother to do everything, but she was wonderful and managed, with a little help from Jutta and me. Spring came and with it a bright array of delicate and sweetly-smelling flowers. The balmy air felt good and there was a new freshness which put a spring into our steps. Then the air raids picked up in intensity, with bombing by both day and night, some destined for Eisenach but mostly overflying to towns and destinations beyond. The American bomber would often fly in fairly low, in daylight, and shoot into the crowds. There were frequently many casualties because invariably the planes would arrive with little or no warning. The alarms would be sounded so late that the people had insufficient time to take cover before the aircraft were overhead. It was carnage.

One day I had to run an errand for my mother. As I walked round a corner into a wide avenue, I was confronted by American planes flying straight towards me as if guided in on wires to the street on which I found myself. They flew in so low with their machine guns blazing that it seemed only a few escaped the hail of bullets. Then the bombs started to rain down, and it was one big massacre, because everyone had been caught out in the open with no advance warning from the sirens. Realising my peril, I raced into the nearest shop and shouted for help, but everyone there was hastily retreating to the cellar. I was terrified by the noise and screams from outside, and blundered my way downstairs following an old lady who was having difficulty negotiating the steep treads. When the ordeal was over and the drone of the aircraft had died away into the distance, we all slowly emerged from our shelter. As my eyes adjusted to the bright light outside, I saw that out in the streets there was total mayhem. People were lying in the road, many of them severely injured, and some of them children. Some had been hit by falling masonry from the surrounding buildings, and there was much crying and moaning. Blood bespattered stonework and the roadway, and I recall seeing a severed arm lying amongst the devastation. Ambulances arrived within a very short space of time and people were running everywhere. The vivid scenes that I witnessed that day became imprinted upon my memory. I forgot all about my mother's errand and ran home as fast as I could. My mother was so overjoyed to see me home safe and sound that she completely forgot the small task which had taken me out onto the streets in the first place.

The war switched its attention to other cities and the attacks on and over Eisenach eased considerably. Heavy damage was reported from raids launched against Bremen, including severe damage to the Gestapo headquarters the thoughts of which gave us great pleasure. The raids on Eisenach however, had left 5,300 homeless and largely at the mercy of the elements. If they could not find friends to take them in they perished. The winter raged on through until February when it unleashed its ferocious worst. All the toilets became frozen and no one was able to have them mended or to prevent them freezing up again after any brief thaw. Our kitchen was so cold that in the mornings there were sheets of ice formed from frozen condensation. Some mornings my mother would advise us to stay in bed, huddled together for warmth, and she would bring us a hot water bottle – if water was available. The pipes could be frozen up, or the water might not be able to get through from the reservoirs because of a blockage or a broken main. Every drop of water had to be conserved to enable us to cook, drink and wash. It didn't matter if your household was rich or poor – money couldn't guarantee the availability of this most essential of commodities and everyone had to muddle through as best they could.

The NSDAP had been fairly accommodating and reasonable in their dealings with my father and had given him considerable time to think over their proposal that he divorce my mother. His period in the Concentration Camp was perhaps a warning of what could happen, the application of pressure to try to make him change his attitude; but it seemed unlikely that they would simply ignore my mother's Jewish roots, having discovered them. We were conscious that their patience would not last forever and that matters were likely to become trickier with every passing month. In the meantime we were not forced to wear the "Yellow Star" and tried to continue our lives as normally as possible. My mother carried on the business with a forced smile and a heavy heart; and Jutta and I continued our studies at the High School.

Something was afoot however. We were increasingly aware of the children's hostility towards us, and the teacher told them not to become too friendly with us. The children stopped talking to us, and one day someone drew my face on the blackboard and started laughing and pointing at it and then at me. The teacher also began ignoring me and when I put up my hand to answer a question she would never acknowledge my existence. One afternoon we formed up into a queue to show the teacher the results of our embroidery and sewing endeavours. She started to praise my work saying that it was an excellent piece: but she then glanced up, saw whose effort it was and started pulling at it and saying it was rubbish.

On another occasion, the Herr Director of the School sent for me and asked, "Why is your English so much better than the others? Have you relatives in England or America? Have they given you extra tuition?" My parents had warned me that in such circumstances I should say I hadn't, so I meekly responded "No, Herr Director!"

believing least said, soonest mended. The trouble was that the aggravation at school only got worse and worse. Our school had had many Jewish children amongst its pupils but most of these had been deported a long time ago.

In our class there was one girl who I considered to be a good friend, and one day she suddenly broke down and burst into tears in the middle of the lesson, sobbing her heart out. The teacher was very nasty to her saying, "Don't be a little cry baby. Stop your blubbering, and tell the class why you are so distraught. You're a silly little girl. Come on now. Tell everyone what is so terrible that you've got to disrupt my class like this." My friend didn't, but she later told me that that very morning the Gestapo had seized her father as he was about to leave the house, her mother having been taken away two days previously. Understandably, she was feeling very alone and afraid. A neighbour of hers had agreed with her parents that they would take her in and look after her, but her grief was beyond control. She never saw her parents again and, when I met her after the war, she told me that she learned that both of them had perished in a concentration camp.

Spring arrived but little changed. The shortages and the bombing of surrounding towns became more incessant, and there were few occasions for rejoicing. Our one comfort was that we were still in our home, together as a family. Our shop had been regularly attended by two boys from the Hitler Youth. They watched everyone who entered the shop and if they did not use the "Heil Hitler" greeting, they took their names and addresses and later reported them. We got quite used to their antics after a while, but wondered how long the status quo could last. One customer who used to come regularly to the shop was Karl, a professional boxer who, one day early in 1943, pulled my mother to one side and informed her that, just like us, the Nazis had their eye on him and his family. Karl's family were all Communists and he believed it was imperative that both our families escaped the regime before it was too late. It was arranged that he would come round to our house that night in order to discuss the matter further.

Although the Jews were the main target for the Nazis' persecution, others such as the Communists, Jehovah's Witnesses, gypsies and the mentally ill, were all included in their "final solution" policy. Few knew exactly how this was being achieved and information was usually hearsay with few concrete facts. A gentleman with whom we were friendly obtained from somewhere a newspaper published in Switzerland, and we were shocked to learn what was happening to those who did not conform to the "Aryan" ideal. It was reported that over 2 million Jews had been killed in villages and ghettos, a figure which was to rise to 6 million – more than half Europe's pre-war Jewish population, by the time hostilities ceased. We read that many were shot down at mass murder sites, and many more were forced from their homes and taken to camps in Poland where they were starved or beaten to death. Some were made to work outside during the winter and in snow with only light clothing to keep them warm – they froze to death. It seemed almost incomprehensible that such inhumanity could really be happening.

When my father came home on a short period of leave from working in the Fire Brigade, my mother told him of the gruesome and diabolical atrocities which she had read were being perpetrated by the Nazis. He agreed to a meeting with Karl, who owned a large swimming pool complex out of town in a nearby village called Mosbach. There were six changing rooms, three for women and three for men. It was proposed that these cabins be converted into two family rooms and that they be fitted with a chimney so that we would be able to cook. After an evening's discussion of the various practical considerations and the problems associated with its implementation, my father agreed to the plan and Karl set about organising everything himself. The main drawback to the proposals was the fact that we would be unable to put them into full effect until the close of the 1942 summer season when the pool would be mothballed for the coming winter. Could we wait that long? Would the Nazis come for us before then?

Karl worked on the cabins when he could during the spring and summer, but time was running out. He and his family were being questioned more and more, and it was clear that we would have to make our move soon. One afternoon a gentleman came to see my mother, the same one who had come once before to tell us of my father's incarceration in Buchenwald Camp. "I come again as a friend," he said. "I must warn you that you have all been placed on a list for deportation. It is imperative that you get away and go into hiding now." As my mother ushered him from the shop she thanked him profusely for his warning and advice. What was churning through her mind at that time I do not know but she showed no outward sign that she was unduly worried.

The following day, however, my mother noticed that nobody entered the shop. When she looked outside two boys, dressed in Hitler youth outfit turned people away who tried to enter the shop. My mother panicked and ran to our school. Luckily, we were on our breaks. When my mother saw me, she told me to come home at once without being seen. She raced to the other class where my sister was and without hesitation we all ran, as fast as we could back home. The shop was closed for good and we started packing. My father was called to serve in the Fire Brigade, which was a good distance away from our home. It was difficult to get in touch with him, therefore she went to see a good friend of ours and pleaded with him to help getting my father out. These people owned a restaurant where we frequently went for our dinner. Since he had a good amount of Nazi customers there he confided in one of his friends who dined there regularly. He asked him if he could help to get my father out for a few days. He told us that my father was not in the Fire Brigade but interned, namely imprisoned.

I do not know how he managed it but my father was able to come home. We were very grateful for his help. My father was happy and he arranged the move to Mosbach, where Karl had already arranged the rooms for us to stay and for his family. My mother packed our handcart with bedding, clothes and other essential items, most importantly some food, whilst my father picked up his briefcase containing important documents.

Neighbours watched and wanted to know where we were going. It was a long walk, which took us two hours, mainly uphill. In the early days, our home had harboured such wonderful and treasured memories for us all that it seemed improper to be deserting it at this stage. It was folly for us to stay there any longer though.

I don't think I've ever seen my father so nervous as he was in these new and somewhat unreal surroundings. My mother tried her best to settle us down into our new accommodation, but my father would stand forlornly at the small window and gaze out, not really seeing what was there. He became withdrawn and had little to say. He became lost in his own thoughts not having the normal activities he was used to. He was worried for the future and became more and more obsessed with the thoughts that our hideout might be discovered. Effectively we had broken cover and now we were living on our wits, fearful that the authorities would learn of our location. My father had nothing in common with Karl and his family, which included three children and with a fourth due at any time. They were not even our friends and we were merely all thrown together by the circumstances of our predicament. Living together in such cramped quarters with boisterous children forever under our feet, led to some friction and we were all conscious that should anything go wrong with the imminent birth nobody could be summoned to help. We all hoped that there would be no complications.

The changing rooms hideout in Mosbach that we tried to make home

There was only one stove in spite of the fact that Karl had managed to create two separate family rooms. Consequently, my mother and Karl's wife took it in turns to cook for both families and we all ate together. However, as far as we were able we tried to avoid lighting the stove for fear that the smoke would give us away. It seemed to rain virtually every day, mercilessly and unceasingly. It was also very cold, but as the days went by we were all reasonably happy, making the best we could of an unsatisfactory situation. The rations of food we took with us did not last a long time. We had no ration cards any more. My mother sent me to the village nearby to buy some bread, milk and eggs. All these items were rationed, and only obtainable by black market. My mother had to exchange expensive jewellery for food, otherwise we would not survive. Karl had ration cards and he did not have to worry. They often shared their food with us. We were very grateful to them, especially for the hide-out. My father suggested to go into the town to our house and collect some of our clothes and food. The idea was not practical but dangerous in any case. My father could not risk it, as he never returned to his interned place. He was sure they were looking for him. Finally, my mother agreed and went.

She took her bike and cycled to our house. Nobody saw her because it was early in the morning. Just as she came out of the house she heard her name calling, and as she turned round she saw her old friend Elsie. Elsie was half-Jewish, and my mother was surprised that she was still around. However, she confided in her that they are leaving the town.

"We are going to Stettin, because it is safer there," she said happily to my mother. "I could take one of your children with me and take her to your mother in Kolberg."

We considered this, but my father was not too happy about it. Time was running out, because her friend was soon leaving. They agreed to meet again and my mother was all in favour because her mother lived on her own. Then one day it was agreed and I asked to go.

At least my parents knew that I would be safer with my Grandmother than there. It was a very sad parting as we did not know if we would see each other again. The train journey took several hours. As we travelled towards Berlin there was an air raid and we had to interrupt our journey to run into a cellar. We both were nervous and I was frightened in case questions were asked by some officials. Everywhere were Nazis, Soldiers, Officials and thousands of people running here and there. Finally, we continued our journey and arrived in Kolberg. Elsie stayed overnight and then travelled to Stettin to her family. My Grandmother was overjoyed to see me. At last, I was safe here. I spent happy days with her, helping her with housework, going on errands, and most of all I kept her company. She was not so lonely now. Spring and summer was not far away and it got warmer. My grandparents owned a few acres of land, where both of us spent a lot of time. It was a lovely garden with fruit trees and bushes. Lovely flowers, and it also had a fish pond. We wondered how my parents were getting on and if they were safe.

Chapter 5
The Gates of Hell

Spring went and summer came with lovely hot weather, and everybody rushed to the beach. However, my happiness did not last long. It was on a brilliant summer's day in 1943. My Grandmother was on an errand whilst I stayed at home; there was a knock at the door.

I was in the kitchen when I heard some shouting and talking, and then, a second knock, only louder. I ran to the window and saw people gathering near our house, and two SS men in their black uniforms. I panicked and tried to hide somewhere under the table, trembling and crying. If only Grandma would come back now from shopping, I prayed. It was no use, because I did not want them to break the door down.

I walked to the door and asked nicely "What do you want? My grandmother is not here!" They all laughed and made jokes about me and my Grandmother. "You come with us, little Jew." I shouted then and said I am not leaving here until my Grandmother returns. They didn't take any notice and manhandled me and pushed me towards a wagon. A few more people were also sitting in the wagon. We were not allowed to talk. Some woman with their children were crying and very frightened. I could not understand this, because Elsie told us that Kolberg was a safe place to be.

They took us to the station and we were eventually pushed cruelly into a freight wagon, which was dirty, smelly and there was nowhere to sit. I had nothing to eat, but some strangers took pity on me and gave me some bread and cheese. The Ukrainians who guarded us were brutal. They shouted and demanded jewellery and money (Zlotys). People who had some money got away without beatings and were allowed a little water. There was only one toilet, which was already full to the brim. Many had to relieve themselves as they were standing. I had no idea where I was going and kept on asking, because it took hours. With the beating, the hunger and thirst I fainted.

We travelled a long time. Now and again the train would stop. Then I noticed through a ridge of the window that the Red Cross suddenly appeared and ran to us give us some food. That was the last time we had anything to eat. The train rolled on and on. I slept and slept and worried about my Grandmother and of course of my parents and sister. Finally, after days of journey we approached a station. It looked like an ordinary station. There was a road to the chambers (I did not know this at that time), planted with small trees, but still we didn't know anything. All at once the truck was opened and we were hauled out.

Many were already dead. It was chaos! People screamed and cried. An entrance off to the left giving access to a luggage room, or so it was labelled. At the back of a waiting room I could see a brightly painted clock which seemed out of keeping with the general squalor of its surrounding. Even so, the clock had a cracked face and the hands were motionless.

This was Treblinka.

Whilst there was a lot of shouting, and screaming from the SS I noticed piles of clothes and shoes. I did not understand. Everybody brought all their belongings they could carry. Sacks, bags and suitcases. I came with nothing. Then they were ordered to leave their belongings behind and then we were herded into groups. I kept away from sight and hid among all those people.

First of all, I heard that the sick, disabled and old people had to stand on one side. Then the young men and women on the other side, who had the task to work, and hopefully to survive. The men had the task to pick up the bundles of clothes, which were left in one big heap, and then take them to the sorting place, where I had the luck to help there. The rest of the people were sent to gas chambers, where their life ended.

Some of the men who were selected to work had been given the task to shave the hair of the victims. So many beautiful women with lovely hair! The hair was actually used for raw materials, like filling mattresses and padding saddles for the cavalry. I couldn't believe my luck when the shaving of hair and tattooing had stopped. There were men who were dentists and they had to extract their victim's teeth, mainly gold teeth. Doing this job meant survival.

The Nazis also chose young people, a special Commando team to clean the road after every transport. The Ukrainians woke us at 4am every morning and we had to work until 6 or 8 p.m. At midday we had to go to the kitchen for our midday meal, which consisted of very watery soup and a little stale bread. Nobody had a choice. If you didn't eat it you would starve.

I was made to help in the laundry, where I worked with an older woman. The work was hard and the long hours made me feel tired and sick. The heat was unbearable we had little to drink. We were plagued by persistent flies and fleas one could not get rid of. There was no standard of hygiene, it was a filthy place and stank. So many prisoners found it impossible to carry on in the heat. They were beaten and made to work harder and harder, so they decided to hang themselves. If they fainted they were beaten to death or even shot. With the arrival of new people, the musicians were called to cheer them up with jolly music. Often the musicians had to stand for hours to play. Many older people and those who were sick and could not walk any more were taken to a Lazaret. They all thought to get care and attention.

The SS ordered them to undress and then were covered with blankets and shot.

The Uprising

We were told that wagons with 2000 prisoners arrived daily. Only lately, fewer wagons arrived. Then we heard rumours that the Red Army would soon come to free us from this place. We hoped but it did not happen.

There were approximately 100 SS men and Ukrainians, but maybe more. The kitchen, workshops, bakery and laundry were opposite sleeping-quarters. The sleeping quarters which were made of wooden structures was for the SS men.

One of the last transports to arrive included several members of the Warsaw Ghetto Underground. They smuggled grenades and pistols beneath their clothing. There was a youngish man on the last transport who knew of an escape plan. At night the men were meeting with this man when he introduced himself. They talked in whispers at night.

This was their plan. Somebody had to get the key from the weapon store, then a copy had been made in the workshop by one of the skilled prisoners. This, we learned turned out to be successful, and the key was then returned.

A young boy, maybe 12 or 14 years old offered to help. First, it was debated that he would be too young for this task, but he insisted and entered the Ukrainian guardroom at night, then stole the weapons, bullets, machine guns, axes and pliers. It was a miracle nobody was to detect anything. Only a few prisoners knew the exact date and time of the uprising to come. They took a big risk. First, they asked him how many should take part, but the leader of the prisoners answered sternly: "All of you!"

My friend, Marushka, who always looked after me in the laundry, calmed me down and said: "We will go together when it happens." Finally, the day had come. The moods of the prisoners seemed to change. They looked happier somehow. Little did we know what was going to happen after our midday meal. Late in the afternoon we heard gunshots, and from the camp further on more shots were fired. Surely, this was the start of a riot, I thought. We were so frightened not knowing what would happen next. Grenades, bottles of petrol exploded, setting buildings on fire.

The Ukrainians and the SS went mad and came running with their rifles, shooting, but many were thrown back with the smoke which surrounded them. The men blew up the Gas Chambers. Next all telephone wires were cut.

The guard in the watchtower had been caught unaware. A cloud of smoke rose from the burning bodies. The flames spread to the SS barracks and other buildings, the death camp Treblinka began to burn. Different smoke from what we saw the previous day – the smoke of martyrdom. A revolt had broken out in the camp. The obtained axes and pliers obtained from the guardroom at night before were now used and handed out.

Different smoke – the uprising

They cut through barbed wire and tried to scramble over the fence. Some tried to push through to the already cut wire, many climbing over the bodies. When the flames spread, hundreds of prisoners were trapped. The SS were firing anywhere where people tried to escape. It was chaos! I was so frightened, not knowing what to do and looking out for my dear friend. With the oncoming smoke I was not able to see. Then one of the lads came running, shouting and dragging me along towards the fence. I shouted back: "I cannot do it!" He pushed me further, and I struggled through the already cut fence, but my dress got entangled with the wire.

"Please help me!" I cried. The men pushed me through as hard as they could to avoid rifle shots. I fell, but quickly got up and started to run. I was out of the camp at last. I didn't see my dear friend, but could not wait. Blood was running down onto my legs, my dress was torn and I was bewildered at what to do and where to run to. I had no choice but to run for my life.

The Ukrainians ran after everybody who escaped and I heard shots all the time. I knew they were still in the forest running after prisoners. Slowly the forest thinned and fields allowed me to make faster progress. The little roads seemed to go on endlessly. I had not realised how arduous my flight would be and I began to doubt whether I could survive the night if I could not find shelter before darkness fell. Out of nowhere, a dog started to follow me. I was terrified but he kept by my side.

I knew very little about Treblinka and its surroundings. My knowledge being only of the camp itself. The camp was around 1.0 to 1.5 kilometres from the River Bur; although whether I was heading towards it or away from it I had no real idea. I knew Ostrow and that there were several villages.

I was crying now silently as I didn't know what to do next. I was bleeding from scratches imparted by the brambles and thickets, in addition to what had happened getting through the fence I had escaped through. I decided to knock on a peasant's door. I was not able to speak in Polish. I tried to explain, but in vain. The door was slammed in my face.

I carried on and tried other houses, but nobody helped me. One lady came to the door and when she saw me she gave me some bread and sausage which I ate with great thanks and left. To my dismay I heard the growing rumble of heavy army trucks some distance away. In the distance I saw a farmyard. I ran quickly before I could be seen.

I buried myself in a pile of stacked hay within one of the barns. It was a joy to see two little cats curiously looking up to me. I fell asleep. I was exhausted. The growing rumble of army trucks settled and a silence and tranquillity returned. I slept for hours and in the early hours of the morning. When I woke in the morning the dog was gone. One of the farmhands spotted me and shouted: "What are you doing there?"

Then I cried and cried and pleaded him to help me, although he didn't understand me and I did not understand him. I must have looked a sorry sight as I crawled out. My clothes and the expression of desperation on my face gave it all away. Hay stuck to my hair and my dress to the general dirt and wet filth I had picked up during my escape. He was beckoning for me to come forward, and then wanting me to come with him. One of the farm workers, called Franek, was able to speak a little German, and introduced me to his mother. She was so nice and helpful and offered to help me to get washed. She washed my hair which was engrained with dirt and fleas and then gave me some breakfast. Franek's father was the head of the family, who owned the farm. His name was Josef Stanislaw. They had two daughters, called Maria and Helena. They told me I was not safe there. If the Nazis found out they were hiding me they would be shot. What was I going to do?

At last they came up with one idea, namely to hide me in the cellar. I agreed, because what else could I do? Where could I go to? The houses and farms were always searched in this area, they told me. I knew they took a risk hiding me.

Josef, the father, took me to the cellar, which was divided into three distinct parts. On the left hand side was a storage area for the coal and logs, and on the right hand side was a section of the wall of which carried many shelves. On these were ranged a vast number of glass jars in a variety of shapes and sizes. Most of them contained marmalade, jams, vegetables and all kinds of fruits, all carefully preserved or pickled through arduous labours of the farmer's wife and their two daughters.

I wondered whether this was where he wanted me to hide. He smiled at me and then pushed against the blank stone wall. Slowly it gave to his pressure and swung open.

"We shall hide you in here," he said with a smile. Would you like to do this? Of course I gladly agreed, thinking the war should be over soon. Everything was prepared for me, bedding and warm clothes of course.

I was not allowed to leave my refuge because there was the ever present danger that one of the lorries which trundled past at frequent intervals, might turn off the road outside and the place be searched. I saw very little daylight throughout that winter as my subterranean hidey-hole afforded me no glimpse of the outside world. Indeed, the passage of time for me was not measured in terms of the rising and setting of the sun, but by the comings and goings of the family as they brought me food at regular intervals. Time hung heavily but always I was thinking about my mother, my father and my sister. I wondered if they had had to suffer, whether they were alive or dead, and what they might be doing at that very moment. Maybe they were thinking about me too.

Christmas 1943 was nearly upon us and there was a heightened degree of activity and urgency upstairs. Maria and Helena often came to see me, to sit with me, and to talk. We could not understand each other at all well, but the companionship was warming and we were able to laugh together from time to time. One of the farm labourers employed by the Stanislaws, Stefan, came too, and I especially looked forward to his visits because he did understand German fairly well. He told me stories of his native Poland, taught me some of its history, and filled this young girl's heart full of dreams and hopes. He spoke of the famous salt mine in Wilichka, of the church and statues made out of salt alone, of the brooks and rivers of Poland the largest of which is Vistula, of the mountains and his excursions onto the oldest in Europe, Zrakopane, and of his abhorrence of what was currently happening to his beloved homeland. He effused about Poland with a nationalist fervour and taught me so much that I had not learned during my early life there.

I hoped to be able to visit my birthplace again once the war was over, and I told him of my family and how I was brought up in the early years of my life in the small seaside resort of Kołobrzeg. I painted verbal pictures of the clean white beaches washed by the Baltic Sea, the peaceful atmosphere, our house, and playing with my school friends in an untroubled world. The innocence of youth protects the young from realising the enormity of events which can be going on around them. I spoke of my nonchalant acceptance, as a nine-year-old, of my father's announcement that we would have to leave Kołobrzeg, and my vivid memories of our departure, the upheaval of leaving school and friends, and the settlement of our family in the new business venture in Eisenach, Thuringia. I told

Stefan of things that I had not discussed with anyone before and of my desire to return there immediately after the war, because I was convinced that that was where my family would all be reunited. We talked a lot about our hopes and aspirations but there were times when I despaired of ever returning anywhere. In my lonely exile I clung to Stefan's visits and talked and talked to put off his departure. Then, when he was gone, I longed for the time he would return and we could converse and dream some more.

When Christmas Day arrived I was allowed to go upstairs and join the family in the dining room. Everything was so festive, and there was a spontaneity about the gaiety and celebrations. The winter had come with added severity again this year, and for me it was a real delight just to sit near a blazing fire, gazing into the flickering and dancing flames. I dare not think of what might be happening back in the Camps. Christmas had always been a special time for me and my family, and as I joined my Polish friends in their celebrations, my thoughts turned in heartfelt rending, to remembrances of Christmases past and to hopes for Christmases yet to come.

The village seemed especially quiet, and the traffic on the road outside was virtually non-existent. It was as if we were in another world, isolated in our own little cocoon that the rest of humanity had forgotten. We all said our prayers together, offering up thanks for all our blessings and then, after I'd returned to my hideout in the cellar, the whole family left for the local church.

I had always known Christmas as a time of goodwill and peace, and I could not see the need to stay cooped up in my cellar when there was a lovely fire roaring in the hearth upstairs. After all, even the soldiers would lay down their arms and stop shooting at Christmas time. I opened the door of my refuge and climbed the stairs to the dining room. I did not realise that the Nazis were not interested in Christmas and that it had no meaning to them – that they would be carrying on their duties in the same way.

Suddenly, I became aware that all was not still and peaceful outside, that there was a lot of shuffling and shouting, dogs were barking and there were other general noises of commotion. I peeped round the edge of the window and saw Germans, lots of Germans, with dogs. Armed soldiers were standing in the roadway, some even just inside the farm-yard, but all were looking towards the house on the other side of the road. They had broken down the front door and were conducting a search. I'd been foolish. I fled down the stairs, taking the steps two at a time. My heart was pounding like mad. If they had come to this house first or been around when I'd first emerged into the empty house the story could have been very different. I raced into the cellar and crept through the little hole in the wall into my hiding place. The door was heavy and on this occasion it seemed even heavier – normally one of the family would open or close the door for me. After some considerable effort, I managed to close it and hid in the farthest corner, I curled up to make myself as inconspicuous as possible. I knew however that if they discovered the door and opened it there would be no escape.

This visitation by the Germans rekindled all the old fears which over the past month had started to recede. My heart was beating so fast; I was feeling sick. I could hear dull noises from outside as presumably they searched the outbuildings. I was fairly confident that they would not have heard me in my mad scramble to regain my sanctuary, but they had been moving around outside for quite some time when I heard the voices of Maria and Helena who presumably had just returned from church. They were followed fairly closely by their mother and father, who were challenged by the Germans. I was not able to hear much but undoubtedly there was a lengthy conversation in progress. Then the voices started moving around and getting louder, so a search must have been underway. Were they looking for me, I wondered? It was approximately a month since I'd escaped and they had surely missed me from the camp before now. Though, to leave it a month before initiating a house to house search, did not seem very likely. However, whether they were looking for me or just searching generally, the outcome of discovery would be the same.

I tried to squeeze myself further into the corner and hugged my legs to try and prevent myself from shaking. My heart was pounding so hard I wondered if they might hear it.

Now they were in the cellar. I could even hear the sniffing of the dogs and the faint sounds of talking. All the time they were separated from me by just a small door. What if someone decided to lean against it? I thought my time had come. How could they possibly miss it? I trembled, I shivered, but most of all I prayed.

I had the best Christmas present I could have received that Christmas day. My prayers were answered, and the Germans departed, although not empty-handed. Josef gave them a goose for their Christmas dinner, and a few bottles of spirit or wine with which to wash it down. The soldiers shook hands with the family and laughed and joked in a good-humoured way, thinking they had found some good friends in this farmer and his family. Little did they know that it had all been an act for me – to send them happily on their way and to dispel any thoughts they might harbour that another visit might prove more worthwhile. Maria came down and told me all this as soon as they felt that the danger had passed. She took me in her arms because the experience had so unnerved me that I was almost petrified with fear. As we sat there in the corner she told me that her father was satisfied that the Germans would not return and that I had nothing to fear now. At the time I gave no thought to her feelings during the search, but her whole family must have been just as relieved as I, when the Germans did not find me.

Christmas passed and with the coming of the New Year, the winter grew more ferocious. Snow and ice built up, paralysing much of the immediate area. It turned freezing cold and down in my cellar which had become surprisingly damp, probably from my own expiration, I became very ill. The Stanislaws decided that I had to come out of the cellar if I was to survive. I was carried up into the warm living room and for several nights slept on the sofa. I had an infection on my lungs and my breathing became laboured and weak. It was impossible for a doctor to be called to tend me, and Mrs. Stanislaw did everything in her power to pull me through. This was a very worrying time for all of them, and I could see the concern etched on their faces. I was given steam baths and herbal teas, I was pampered and nursed with the tenderest of love, and I could not have been treated with more care if I'd been one of their own children.

The air raids grew in length and frequency during January and February 1944. As I listened to the planes flying overhead, my spirit was lifted and I felt happier, because all the indications were that the war was entering its final death throes. As soon as my health permitted, I returned to the cellar, and had to rely then on the messages that the family brought down to me. Josef came down one day and said, "It will not be long now, Anneliese. The war is almost over." I smiled back at him and hoped that he was right. His words though started me wondering yet again whether my parents had survived this far and whether I would see any of my family again. One Sunday morning in early April the noises of over-flying bombers started really early. I went up with the family to see what was happening. The sky was full of planes, orderly lines of planes flying ponderously overhead, the sun glistening on their under-bellies. There were more planes than I could ever have imagined, and the ground shook and trembled under our feet as the vibrations and sound from so many engines reached down out of the sky to jangle our senses. In the distance we could see increasing columns of smoke climbing up into the sky, and on the road, traffic, limited as it was, all seemed to be in one direction.

This was surely the beginning of the end. How could people take such punishment? Maybe tomorrow this terrible war will come to its long-awaited end. Maybe tomorrow I, along with everyone else, will be able to taste and experience freedom once again, to walk without fear into the daylight and sunshine. Maybe. For now, though, it was back to my 'prison' in the cellar.

During March and much of April it rained relentlessly, as if even nature itself was crying for all the hurt we were doing to ourselves. Night and day the rain came down, flooding the streets and drowning the fields. Until one day, it dawned sunny and warm. I awoke suddenly alerted by a lot of activity above. I heard the outer door to the cellar open and I jumped up from my creaking sleeping accommodation, my eyes fixed on the door to my inner sanctuary. What has happened? Have they found me? Are they searching again? My thoughts were in overdrive and my heart was pounding so loud that anybody nearby would have been able to hear it. I was cold with fear. I said a prayer. Anything that came into my head. I called out all the names of the saints that I could remember, to Our Lady and to Judas Thaddaeus, helper in all difficult situations. I heard voices, but no male voices.

Strange. I dressed quickly, just in case. The Nazis would have dragged me out and not allowed me the time to throw some clothes on. Now the footsteps are coming nearer. Who could come at this time? I glanced at the little clock on the small wooden table which Fran had given to me at Christmas. It was nearly 7.30 a.m. This was too early for breakfast. Helena normally brought it down around 8.30 a.m. Suddenly the heavy door swung open and there stood Maria, her face lit up in the broadest of smiles and her arms flung out towards me. She brought me the good news that the Germans had pulled out, driven back by advancing Russian troops. It was my birthday: 2nd June – what a birthday present.

I no longer had to hide and could live a more normal life, helping on the farm and in the kitchen, waiting for a time when it was safe to resume my life back home.

Maria also brought me the news in May 1945.

"Come on, come on, quickly" she said, her voice full of happiness. She got hold of me and then swung me round and round.

"Stop it. Stop it," I shouted. "You are making me dizzy." She carried on laughing and laughing.

"What has happened? Please tell me," I pleaded.

"I have some stupendous news," she said joyously.

"Good news?" I enquired, fixing her with a quizzical gaze.

"The war is over," she said in Polish, but it was difficult to understand her and her sign language. I wanted to believe what I thought she was saying but I was not going to trust my emotions until I was sure of her meaning. Helena then came to me in the cellar and without a word, led me by the hand up into the bright sunlight which was streaming through the windows of the farmhouse and bathing the yard outside in its brilliant rays. The sunlight dazzled my eyes and I was temporarily blinded. I still could not be confident of their intentions and thought the Nazis might have found me. I pulled against her frightened of what she might be taking me towards. "Anneliese, my dear Anneliese," Helena said quietly. "Come. There is nothing to be afraid of. Come with me and just listen." Then I heard the bells. Bells were ringing long and loud. The peels of the local church bells were rebounding and echoing over the landscape, joining up with the sounds of bells from across the whole of the country. A hundred church bells, thousands of church bells, ringing throughout the breadth of the land. What had happened? It must be good news. Stefan caught me up at the doorway, his whole face one broad smile and, embracing me in his huge brawny arms, said, "Anneliese, the war is over. Germany has surrendered to the Allies. Isn't it just wonderful?"

Before I could even reply, he was off and away. I couldn't believe it. I started to shake uncontrollably. People were running everywhere, joy etched across their faces. Dogs were barking and children were excitedly running hither and thither. We were all embracing each other, and Helena and Maria had tears in their eyes. I broke away to give a little dance and twirl in the middle of the yard and let the sun strike me full on the face as I gave thanks for my deliverance. It was 9th May 1945. It was one of the most glorious summer days there had ever been. God had at last answered the prayers of so many of his believers, and had blessed us with the peace for which we had all longed for so long. This was a day on which we could all rejoice and weep tears of happiness and relief. The nightmare was over at last. Now I was able to leave my refuge in the cellar for good. No more lonely nights underground, and no more hiding. I knew that a new chapter of my life was about to unfold and that I would soon need to start laying plans for a return home in search of my family. But first, it was a time for celebration as the villagers gathered together for one huge party. Neighbours and friends came from all around, and there was even a little dancing. Josef brought out some of his best wine for all of us to share and the festivities went on into the night. No-one wanted this joyous day to end.

Epilogue

The camp, called Treblinka was built in 1941 and altogether some 850,000 people of various nationalities were to die here before its liberation, many from the Warsaw Ghetto.

It was one of the four main extermination camps operated by the Germans and had the second largest throughput after Auschwitz. Treblinka was a small town in Polish Silesia at the confluence of the Vistula and Sola rivers and was linked by rail through both Malkinia junction and Siedice with Warsaw district.

Several hundred prisoners were able to break out of the camp, more than half of whom were then traced and killed by Nazi authorities, but some managed to make their way to the forests of Eastern Poland.

After the August 1943 Treblinka Uprising, the SS made the last prisoners plough up the ground and remove all traces; then they were shot. Many had to dig their own graves, and were then buried alive.

Corpses were burned to ashes and traces of crime removed, in order to conceal their crimes in the face of the advancing Red Army. Today a huge memorial stands where the Treblinka Camp once stood.

Chapter 6
My Homecoming

It was at the end of June 1945, just turned 16, that I found myself riding into the outskirts of Eisenach aboard a bumpy ill-equipped lorry, which had been my sole transport all the way from the holding camp in Munich. Since I'd lived here in Eisenach with my parents and sister for over six years, I should have recognised it easily but I was dismayed at how much it had changed in the short time that I had been away. Still it marked the end of my journey, nearly three weeks after I had said my fond farewells to the Stanislaw family.

I was accompanied by a few companions for whom Eisenach had also been home but I did not know any of them and, while we were all bewildered, exhausted, hungry and poorly dressed, there was hope flickering in all of our hears for the homecoming. My thoughts fleetingly turned to the other uncomfortable journeys I had endured as a captive of the Germans and I offered up a prayer for the many people who did not have the good fortune to survive and to return home like me. While there was still a wretchedness about our plight we were very much the lucky ones and had much for which to be thankful.

As our lorry passed by other similarly laden lorries, sight of their pitiful cargoes brought tears to my eyes. There were hundreds upon hundreds of people from the Concentration Camps in those vehicles – emaciated bodies draped in the awful striped garments which labelled them as camp survivors. Mere skeletons who did not have the strength to move. The vast majority were obviously sick and their overall condition was indescribable. It seemed impossible, as I looked in upon them, that some of those frail structures of skin and bone could still be alive.

Our transportation eventually drew up outside a huge building in the town centre, which I instantly recognised as that belonging to the Electricity Supply Company. Given all the damage to the other property in its vicinity it looked remarkably unscathed. We were welcomed by the Americans, who had occupied the town since the beginning of April 1945, and led into the main hall, which was itself all too familiar to me. What was not, were the vast numbers of people milling around, packing it wall to wall. Many were so sick that they had to be transported to hospitals, where they got proper medical care, but for some it was too late and they did not survive.

Everybody was talking, questioning their compatriots, seeking answers from people who were equally unclear as to what was happening. I felt overpowered by the melee but eventually one of the officers in charge called us to order and a silence fell over the throng. We were divided into groups and were requested to complete a series of questionnaire forms. Further questions were then asked of us as we handed over the completed forms, and finally we were given something to eat and drink.

I was ravenous and tucked into my repast with relish, consuming every last morsel. I then leant back, closed my eyes as if in thanksgiving, and just relaxed with relief. I was back in surroundings with which I was familiar and under no pressure to be other than myself. Suddenly, while I was just sitting there I was overwhelmed by my emotions and broke down into uncontrollable crying. An American soldier came up to me and put a comforting arm around my shoulders. "Can I help you in any way?" he asked with a sort of resigned helplessness. I wasn't used to such warmness. "I am all right now thanks," I whispered as I wiped away my tears with an old ragged handkerchief which I'd found tucked away in the corner of one of my pockets. I think it must have been one which Marie had given to me when I was sheltering with her family and it has become one of my most treasured possessions. As I put it back into my pocket I paid greater attention to what was happening around me. It was a long time since I'd seen such healthy and jolly-looking people, and their presence gave sight of the opportunities that lay ahead. I felt that a great weight, which had hung over me for the many months that I'd been separated from my parents, had suddenly been lifted and I sobbed some more as the feelings of relief and the ebbing of the tension under which I had lived for so long, engulfed me.

My English was limited to that which I had learned in school and I found the American accent both strange and difficult to understand. Luckily, there were a few German people who were able to come to my rescue and to assist me, through translation, to have a limited dialogue with the Americans. I pointed out to them that Eisenach was my hometown and that now all I wanted to do was to go home and find my family. They had lists of people who had already arrived and passed through their hands and those who were in transit to other places in the locality, but my parents did not appear on any of these. They made enquiries at other centres but their attempts to locate or obtain information about any of my relatives, proved to be in vain. As the time ticked by with no news, my spirits started to sink and my fears grew that they had perhaps perished or were dreadfully ill somewhere and not fit enough to make the journey home. The Americans assured me however, that not all of the lorries had yet arrived and that it was possible they might be among the later arrivals. Certainly, it was too early to be thinking that they might not come back to join me.

It was well known that the houses in which Jews used to live had been taken over by Nazi families, but I had not anticipated that creating any sort of problem now that Hitler and his regime were no more. Indeed, I had envisaged visiting our old house on the very day that I arrived back in Eisenach and had thought that it would be just as I had left it. I was advised by the Americans to wait until the following morning when they could probably find someone to go with me, a suggestion to which I readily agreed when I realised how weary I was feeling. I stayed overnight in the large reception hall, sleeping where I could, but I was filled with anticipatory excitement and couldn't wait for the dawn to come.

Our house lay a considerable way outside of town and the Officer looking after the reception centre arranged for me to be taken there in one of the American jeeps. A tall and handsome American was detailed to look after me and as he swung his lean frame into the driving seat he fixed me with a broad smile. "Everything is going to be just fine, honey," he assured me. "We'll have you back home in no time." He was really friendly and I suppose when I look back he was probably flirting with me, although at the time I did not realise it. I was preoccupied with thoughts of seeing our house again and, while I was 16 years old, I had lost several years of normal growing up and was still an innocent little girl in such sexual liaisons. He talked a lot but there was little I understood. Indeed, my attention was more upon the immediate surroundings and the littered potholed streets through which he delicately wove the jeep, then upon the ramblings of his drawling voice. Maybe he only wanted to cheer me up but as we drove along I started to day-dream.

The heat was proving unbearable and I was conscious that I would have liked a refreshing wash. It would be lovely when everything was back to normal – whatever that might mean in the immediate post-war period; and I started to dream of the luxury of soaking in a nice warm bath and then dressing in nice clothes and high-heeled shoes. "Which way now?" he suddenly shouted across to me, noticing that my thoughts were far away and not watching the passing landscape. "Up the hill and turn right at the oak tree please," I responded almost automatically, once I'd gathered my senses and located where we were. I was nearly home and my heart was pounding fit to burst. I was fast approaching a moment of truth and just did not know what to expect. Obviously, I hoped my family would be there to welcome me with open arms – but what if they were not?

The jeep screeched to a sudden halt amidst a swirl of dust, and my American GI turned to me and asked me about the name of the street and the number of the house. There was no need. Here it was. We had stopped directly outside. "We are here. Right here", I called as I jumped excitedly from the passenger seat. "But please don't leave me yet, will you? I do not know who, or what, awaits me inside. Your presence out here would boost my confidence." I raced up the few steps and knocked at the so-familiar door. Nobody answered. I stood there trembling, not knowing what to do next. I knocked more urgently but still no one came. It was never like this when I used to skip joyfully home from school. My mother's face swam before my eyes as I recalled how she used to usher me in through the front door and greet me with a hug and kiss. I remembered also other endearing acts with which she used to welcome me home and how sometimes my father would come to the door or would be playing the piano as I crossed the threshold and strolled into the living room. The neighbours used to admire him and invariably there would be welcoming smiles of recognition from them as any one of us approached our house. Today though, nobody was in sight and the front door remained firmly closed.

The American alighted from the jeep and joined me at the foot of the steps where I was by then gazing appealingly up at the dirty windows fronting onto the street. "Nobody is here," I said in answer to his questioning gaze, and thought to myself that my mother could not have returned because she would never have allowed the windows to be in the filthy state. I had knocked several times and I'd even tried the doors around the back of the house as well, but all to no avail. We returned to the jeep where we sat for over an hour in the hope that someone would turn up; but nobody did. I was terribly upset at this anticipated joyous home-coming and became more despondent as the time passed.

A number of German ladies strolled by during our wait and gave us some very cool and unfriendly glances. They were whispering and gossiping and from their general demeanour and frequent looks in our direction, it was very clear that they were talking about us. I didn't care. Eventually I got out of the jeep and went over to a couple who were standing a couple of doorways away from us. "Excuse me," I asked, "but can you please tell me who lives at the house just down there?" I pointed at our house as I continued, "I have been away for so long." They looked puzzled by my enquiry and were curious as to why I should be asking. However, they could not help and suggested I try the house next door. That was not particularly encouraging; but then neither was the fact that I hadn't recognised one of the people who had passed by during our wait nor seen one friendly face. I couldn't understand why so much had apparently changed in the short time which had elapsed since we had been forced to flee. I had deliberately refrained from calling on our immediate neighbours in the next-door house because I knew the occupants of old and was fully aware that when we lived on the street they had been extremely supportive of the Nazis. Indeed, they had been one of the few houses on our street that hadn't been attacked by the Hitler Youth because their son was an avid member. Eventually however, I decided that no other course lay open to me and, with a quick backward glance to make sure my GI friend was still sitting watching from the jeep, I knocked on their door. It was flung open immediately as if the middle-aged fat lady who stood before me had been standing behind the door expecting my visit. She appeared apprehensive, fearful and unfriendly, as first she looked into my eyes and then over my left shoulder at the American. She then returned her gaze to my enquiring face.

"What do you want from me?" she snapped at me, as she drew back thereby allowing me to slip into the hallway. Her well-fed body around which she had tied a gaudy apron that might easily have doubled as a tablecloth, fascinated me, especially after the food paucity which I had known. "I am sorry to trouble you but I am seeking important information and I am hoping that you can help," I muttered. I must have sounded somewhat nervous and insecure, and I certainly felt intimidated by the bulk of the woman before me. When I began to question her about her neighbours and the occupants of the adjacent house in particular, her concern slowly melted away and she started to become more open and helpful. I learned that a nice family of two adults and three children lived there and that regularly they would all go out walking together. She surmised that that was probably the reason for their absence at that particular time and, given the long wait that I had already had, she thought it unlikely that they would be away much longer.

I returned to my American chauffeur friend and we must have waited two or three hours in total before my quarry came into view. We had watched all the family groups which had passed down the street but there was something about this particular unit which told me that these were the ones that I had been eagerly awaiting even before they stopped at the gate, gave us no more than a perfunctory glance and turned to climb the steps to my old front door.

I gave them a short time to settle inside and then, gathering up my courage and my thoughts, I once again strode up the steps and knocked at the weathered and yet still familiar door. It was flung open almost immediately by the buxom woman I'd seen entering only minutes earlier and she ushered me into the hallway where I explained that I wished to have to talk to her. We chatted for a long time, her husband joining us after discreetly despatching the children upstairs, and she expressed deep concern for my plight and real sorrow for the experiences to which I had been subjected. She offered to let me stay with them until my parents were found but this was one proposal I had no intention of accepting. This had been my house and as far as I was concerned it still was. I was not going to accept an invitation to stay there from strangers whom I considered had no right to be there and were occupying the premises illegally. It was my house.

I went back out to the jeep and to my American friend, who was leaning back against the bonnet soaking up the sun. He had been so very patient and understanding throughout the lengthy visit and I was full of thanks as he drove me back into town and to the Electricity Supply building. I was chattering to him all the way back complaining about the people in my home and how he would have to throw them out. However, I was not sure of my position because I had no papers or documents to support my assertions. I was in something of a panic because I had not thought about what I should do in such circumstances. I had no job, no food, no house, and no family. Nothing. As soon as we pulled up at the reception centre, I was out of the jeep without turning to thank my patient companion and went running inside determined to confront the German officials trying to smooth the traumatic return of refugees and displaced persons to their homes. I rushed up to the table at which two Eisenach Town Hall staff were trying to process a stream of enquiries from a crowd of people gathered around them. I pushed my way to the front and told them about my plight. "First of all," they said, "we need to investigate this matter thoroughly, to validate your statements and to determine your rights to the property. Only then can we consider helping you to take up residence. "I can give you no proof of my claims," I responded. "My father always looked after such matters, but I am sure the neighbours will vouch for my authenticity."

Typically, German, never cutting corners, always so strict for protocol and correctness, I was on the receiving end of a rebuttal to my entreaties. Then one of the gentleman leaned over the desk and said sympathetically, "Have you anybody who knows you and would be willing to put you up while we sort this matter out? A relative or a school friend perhaps?" "Oh yes," I replied, "I do have a very good friend. Her name is Edith, but her parents were Nazis and they never knew of my background. I don't mean that they would do anybody any harm, and they were always nice to me, but if I go to them now they will surely want to know where I have been all this time."

The gentleman frowned and I could see that he was pondering over the best course of action. "Do you know what I think, Miss Wegner. I think that you should go to these friends of yours and explain to them absolutely everything. If they are friends like you suggest I believe you will have no problems. If you do, then come straight back to me." He continued, "We are in a different world now and people's attitudes have changed dramatically. It will take us a few days to sort your papers and I suggest you stay with them and return here at the end of the week." I nodded as if in a dream. I was thinking of Edith and her family. I didn't know how I was going even to begin to tell them my story. Would they be disgusted? Shocked? Sorry? All these things shot through my head as I murmured a profuse "Thank you" and turned to walk pensively from the building. My homecoming was not proceeding as I had imagined.

Chapter 7
Reunion

I plucked up courage for the coming confrontation as I walked slowly towards their hotel, the "Hotel Mille". It was a medium sized hotel with twelve bedrooms for guests, and was owned by Edith's father. Edith's mother had died some years previously and her father had subsequently remarried his wife's sister. She was a highly active, busy, bustling and efficient lady who practically ran the hotel single-handedly. It took me about fifteen minutes to walk to the hotel and, as I approached the huge wooden doors and rang the bell, I wondered what sort of reception I was about to receive. It was mid-afternoon. I heard footsteps. Somebody was coming to the door. It was Edith's aunt. She looked at me and, with a sweeping gesture of her arm, ushered me warmly into the hotel foyer. "Anni, my love, where have you been all this time?" She had always been very talkative and today she jabbered on and on. "I kept saying to Edith we hadn't seen you lately, but she didn't know what had happened to you. Why haven't you come to see us? Edith has missed you. Why, only the other day we were remarking about how we had not seen the Wegner's in their shop for some time. What have you been doing with yourself, young lady?" She paused for breath.

The quick firing of her questions with no room for a reply heightened my anxiety, but I had to tell her something. "You remember when there was all that shooting last summer?" I began. "Well, my father and mother decided that we should go in search of a refuge where we would be safer." Actually, I shouldn't have been telling her anything. I'd promised my father not to breathe a word to anyone and I still felt bound by that promise in spite of the change in circumstances. On the other hand, she was a member of my best friend Edith's family, and I had to offer her some explanation. Besides, a number of people had seen us pushing a handcart laden with a variety of essential household items and I was reasonably sure that that would have filtered through to Edith's family. I recollect that at the time our neighbours had called us cowards for running away, but we couldn't have told them the real truth.

We reached the top of the stairs and she guided me from there into the family's private quarters. Here she turned to me and drew me closely to her in a loving embrace, held me out at arm's length and then hugged me to her again., all the while saying, almost as if she could not believe I was in front of her, "Anni, I am so very glad that you have come back to see us. This was the first hurdle over, I thought to myself. But what about the second part of my story? Sit down, Anni, I am going to fetch Edith. She is somewhere around and she will be overjoyed to see you safe and sound." I felt strange. Would she have hugged me or welcomed me so enthusiastically if she had known the truth about my family.

I was sitting there, fiddling nervously with my fingers, when Edith appeared in the doorway. Her face lit up and she came running across to me immediately with open arms. She hugged and kissed me. "Anni, where have you been all this time? You know you look terrible. Have you not been eating properly? Where are your parents?" she enquired as she held me at arm's length, as if determined to ensure that I didn't get away again. She looked very well. I had never known them to be short of food, and with running a hotel they frequently managed to obtain food which was in very short supply and not available to the vast majority of the populace. She had obviously been living a good life while I'd been suffering – but that was not her fault.

"Edith," I stammered hesitantly. "I have no home. Nothing. Can I stay here with you for a while?" She started to laugh. "What are you talking about Anni? You're talking absolute rubbish. You have a lovely house, a thriving business, and you say you have nothing. Balderdash. Have you been thrown out by your parents? Where are your mother and father?" "I just don't know Edith," I responded in a quivering voice and with a shake of my head. "I just do not know." Then I started to cry and buried my face in the cushions of my chair. I sobbed and sobbed. I could not stop.

Edith's father and Rolf, her brother, came into the room then. "What is going on here?" her father asked rather sternly. There was a pause as I felt tears welling up in my eyes yet again. "Come on my dear Anni, he continued far more soothingly when he had had more time to sum up the situation. "Obviously what you need is something to eat and drink." "Rolf" shouted Edith's aunt from across the room, "lay the table and put the kettle on please. We could all do with a nice break."

Rolf, who was 10 years older than Edith, was always making jokes. Whatever he said in response I did not catch fully but he sang it in a classic type of musical style which brought a smile to my lips. I was beginning to feel better already. Edith's aunt was a proficient cook, as had been her mother when she was alive, and that afternoon she brought out some of her luscious home-baked cakes on a tray. They smelled delicious and tasted every bit as good as they looked. It was really great to be back among my friends of old. The attitude of the German people towards the Jews was still a live issue in many peoples' minds and I didn't know quite how to broach the subject. Certainly I hadn't the courage to tell them my story over the table, there and then. "Where have you been?" enquired Edith for the umpteenth time. "She can tell us all in good time. There is no hurry now," said her aunt. Perhaps she sensed that I was in difficulty.

Edith's father was a very small man, not given to idle chatter, and, as soon as he had finished his coffee, he excused himself and hurried outside to see to his affairs. Go on, Anni," said Rolf, "tell us about it and what has happened to you. Did you get lost in the woods? He was starting to joke and tease me, and I was getting annoyed because he was not helping me find the right atmosphere in which I could feel comfortable elucidating. "No," I said somewhat huffily. I stood up as if I was about to leave. "I am not telling you anything." "Rolf," said Edith's aunt quietly, "leave us for a while please, so that Anni can talk to Edith and me." After he had left the room and I had sunk back into my seat, she turned to me and said in a reassuring and comforting manner, "Well, you obviously want to talk to someone and get something off your chest. We are your friends and want to help you. You are obviously unhappy but you know that you ca talk to us, Anni. Now, how about it?

Are you going to tell us what happened to you, and why you were crying so much earlier this afternoon?"

"Yes," I replied defiantly, "I am going to tell you the whole story, and if at the end of it you want me to leave, then that will be the last you will see of me." Edith and her aunt moved in closer then, and as I unfolded my story they listened more and more intently. There were periods when it was very quiet and the sound of the ticking clock appeared to get louder, but not once did they interrupt my narrative, even though at times I stumbled over my words as I relived some of the horrors in my mind's eye. And so I brought them to my present situation. "I just did not know about this Anni. Why did you never tell me? I was always your best friend." "Yes," I replied to Edith's outburst, after we'd sat briefly looking at each other in silence. "You were my best and dearest friend, and I would like to think you still are, but my parents told me to tell absolutely nobody. We had hoped to survive the war without discovery or internment in a concentration camp. If we have managed that, nobody need every have known of our past."

I suppose I should not have been surprised at how lovely they were towards me following my narrative. I mean, our friendship went back a long way and I should have known it would endure. They insisted that I stayed with them and share Edith's bedroom. They asked if I had any belongings, and when I indicated negatively, Edith took me to her room and pulled out some of her own clothes for me to wear. I had my first good wash for over a week and relaxed contentedly. Edith and I talked into the night, and then I fell into a blissful sleep. The following morning I returned to the reception centre and explained to the German administrators that I would be staying with my friends at the Mille Hotel and that they would be looking after me until the situation regarding my old home could be resolved. They arranged for me to receive a money allowance so that I could pay for my keep, and I returned to the hotel in a much brighter frame of mind. Actually the Americans had commandeered and already occupied all but the bedroom I was in, a second bedroom Rolf shared with his parents, and a small living room, but I hadn't seen them until that morning. They looked very different to the German people and had an appealing vigour. They were tall, broad, handsome, generally fairly young, confident, and the uniforms had especial attraction for me – oh yes, and for Edith. We used to discuss them in the privacy of our bedroom.

Edith had a grand piano of her own and she played classical music with excellent touch and proficiency. She had started to learn when she was only six years old and undoubtedly she had a rare gift. The Americans admired her for her brilliant playing and so they gathered around her to listen. I would think back to those many times, not so long before, when she and my father would sit down together and play duets. They had been marvellous times and I fell to wondering whether they would ever be recaptured. I tried to imagine where my father might be and what my mother and sister might be doing. Surely, one of them would come back to our home in Eisenach on day.

I stayed with Edith's parents for almost a couple of months and each and every day of that sojourn I earnestly sought news of my family. As the days dragged by with no news, however, my spirits slowly sank and I began to despair of ever seeing any of them again. It was only that hope of a reunion which had kept me going since our separation and I had given no thought to a future without my father, my mother and my sister. Such a possibility did not figure in any of my imagined scenarios. While my new "family" were lovely caring people and I was very happy there, nothing could replace my own family and the home life we had shared together. I longed for that day when I could return to my house and be reunited with my family. Often in the evenings, Edith, her family and I would discuss my aspirations, and hope that some cheering news might soon come.

One beautifully sunny morning in late August, a gentleman arrived at the hotel. I was upstairs at the time but could hear voices in the hallway. There was quite a stirring and excitement from downstairs, and then Edith's father shouted up to me. "Anni, come down here a minute, please. There is someone here to see you." I raced down the stairs two at a time and was met by an array of upturned faces. However, I quickly picked out the stranger there and I ran up to greet the kindly-looking gentleman who had a warm ruddy complexion, sparkling blue eyes and a beaming smile which lit up his whole face. "Have you some news for me?" I blurted out, somewhat unnecessarily I suppose in retrospect. "Yes," he said, "Indeed, I have some very good news. Your father has returned and is even now in Eisenach." I couldn't believe it. I jumped up and down with joy. Edith's family all joined in with me in an excited chorus. This was truly fantastic news.

I was so overjoyed and stunned that I was initially lost for words. Then, suddenly, they came gushing forth. "When can I see him? Is my mother with him? Where is my sister?" He was obviously delighted for me, and was overwhelmed by the jabbering and enthusiastic gyrations of an excited youngster. "I am sorry Anni but you must stay here." he responded. "He will come here this afternoon to see you, but do not be alarmed when you see him. He looks very haggard and drawn, but you can rest assured he is all right. It will just take him a little time to regain his strength and old vitality." I danced around, almost singing as I said over and over again: "My father is back. My father is back." Nothing else mattered. What great news. "Oh, I'll have to celebrate this," I joyously said. "Indeed," said Edith's aunt. "We will arrange a coffee-party for this afternoon. I will bake some delicious cakes especially for the occasion and your father will be guest of honour."

The few hours until the reunion dragged interminably and at one minute past midday I could not understand why he had not yet arrived. Within the next hour I must have looked at the clock and dashed to the window at least twenty times. "What can be keeping him?" I kept asking Edith's aunt, who was bustling around making preparations for the afternoon's celebrations. The afternoon dragged on and on, and my glances down the street and to the clock on the wall became more frequent with every passing minute. Two o'clock came and went. Where was he? Then I saw him. He looked older and drawn, but there was no mistaking him. He was walking slowly down the street. I was out of the room and across the pavement, my feet hardly touching the floor. "Papa," I shouted and ran as fast as I could to greet him. He swept me into his arms and we were still standing there when everyone else gathered around to welcome him back. He was smiling now and we strolled back to the hotel in each other's arms. "Has your mother come back? Have you heard anything of her or Jutta?" he enquired, as soon as the immediate euphoria had passed. "No, papa," I replied. "I live here alone with Edith's family who have been kind enough to put me up until I can look after myself." We were ushered into the foyer and all the while I could not take my eyes off him. Sadly, he looked but a shadow of his former self, but he seemed to gain comfort, strength and confidence from our closeness. Tears streaked his face with the sheer joy and relief at having returned and found at least one member of his family alive and well.

Edith's aunt led us into the comfortable living room where she had already laid out a beautiful table for us. It was an exciting moment, this reunion with my father. Many questions were asked, and tentative plans laid. However, my father was obviously very weak and tired, and preferred to leave everything constructive until the next day. Indeed, the day was fast receding and it was late that evening when he returned to the accommodation which had been allocated to him until his affairs could be sorted out. He shook hands with the adults and gave me a long kiss and embrace before departing into the night. I was so excited and didn't think I would every get to sleep. My father was back. I laid in bed and was pondering on how much I had to discuss with him, when I sank into a deep sleep.

Now that my father had returned, efforts to regain possession of both our house and the business were renewed with significantly greater gusto. My father had always seen to the financial aspects of our activities and it was an area about which I knew virtually nothing. This had been his job as the man of the house and he would never allow my mother to interfere in that aspect of their affairs. He used to call at Edith's each morning to see that I was all right and would then go off to progress matters. "Can I come too?" I asked on one occasion. "No," said my father very sternly. "These are things I have to deal with by myself. I need to call upon a lot of different people and you would not find it at all interesting" I naively believed that we would be able to move straight back into our house now that my father had returned but the authorities seemed to be making it as difficult as they could. My father had to prove many things, made all the more difficult because a lot of the written records had been destroyed or gone missing. It became clear that on my own I would not have been able to sort out his affairs. Even so my father became beholden to an old friend of his who gave him considerable assistance and bore witness to the veracity of his statements.

My father after his liberation from Buchenwald

There was a lot to straighten out but because my father didn't confide in me I don't know how it was achieved. For example, I do not know where the money came from to rebuild our lives or to repair our shop in the centre of town. Maybe he still had funds in the bank, or the authorities perhaps made cash available to him. It was an area closed to me. There must have been many people in a similar situation to us who were attempting to rebuild their shattered lives and the agencies trying to smooth out the rehabilitation must have been under considerable pressure. On one of his visits to the hotel, I asked my father somewhat impatiently, "When can we move back into our home, papa?" "Now listen," he replied conciliatorily. "It takes a lot longer than you think. There is much checking and rechecking that has to be done." I was disappointed at the seeming lack of progress – but I still had my good friend Edith as a companion, and her parents were looking after me well. My father unfortunately was living elsewhere in the town and he was not at all happy about that. Still, we laid plans as to what we would do when we moved back into our house and, after all the necessary formalities had been ironed out, we finally got clearance from the authorities.

The other family currently in occupation were made to move and we took up residence in our old home four weeks after my father's return. It took far longer, many months in fact, before our shop was rebuilt and could open for the sale of our specialities of coffee, tea and sweets. We received right of possession at about the same time as the house, but the shop had been so extensively damaged and vandalised that it required a major rebuild. My father put in months of hard work and graft to get the business back on its feet again. I had every confidence in his abilities because I knew him to be a very astute and capable businessman. I was thus never in any doubt that he would achieve his goal, but had not expected it to be 1946 before we were trading. More money was made available and his many friends rallied round and gave us considerable help and understanding during his difficult period of adjustment. My father grew in strength as the days passed but our thoughts frequently turned to the whereabouts of the rest of our family.

Daily we would trek down to the reception centre, hoping against hope for news of my mother and sister, but always it was the same old message. "Sorry, Herr Wagner. There's no news, I'm afraid. Try again tomorrow." My father and I became more and more dispirited, because the steady stream of returning refugees was beginning to tail off. Then, one afternoon late in September, we walked in together and were greeted by a smiling official who said, "Herr Wagner. We have some excellent news for you today. Your wife has been located in a

Leipzig hospital." I am afraid, however that she is very ill and is unable to travel." He continued. It was tremendous news after all the weeks of uncertainty. My father and I immediately made plans to visit her a few days later.

The journey took longer than we had anticipated because, although Leipzig is only 260 kilometres from Eisenach, the train was very slow, stopping at frequent intervals. I suppose our overwhelming desire to see my mother again also meant that the time on the journey seemed to pass more slowly, every stop or hold-up being an unwelcome aggravation and intrusion. I think both of us were apprehensive about meeting her again after such a long time, and wondered how ill she really might be. The people who dealt with lost relatives and friends and had organised the trip on which we were now embarked, had suggested that she was on the road to recovery, but that did not stop us worrying about her well-being. My father was sitting in a corner of the carriage, nervously puffing at a cigar. Every so often he would glance across at me and then, as he turned his head to look out of the window, his eyes would glaze over so that he did not see the passing landscape, because his thoughts were off on a journey of their own. "Can we take mother back with us, Papa?" I asked. "I could look after her, and I'm sure she would like to be home." So deep in thought was my father he could not have heard my questions. Certainly, he did not reply or give any indication that he had understood me. Faced with his apparent wish for isolation, I sank back into my own world of reveries and the journey passed off in an unhealthy brooding silence. Eventually the train arrived at our destination and we alighted into a furore of people scurrying here, there and everywhere. My father grasped my hand to avoid our becoming separated and started to push his way through the crowds. People were shouting, some were laughing, some were searching for relatives or friends, but still seemed to be in a great hurry. There were women with young children, and men with suitcases and baggage, all offering tripping hazards and hazardous obstructions for the surrounding hordes. The natives of this vibrant metropolis all looked so haggard and poorly dressed when compared with the healthy-looking smartly turned-out American soldiers dotted sparsely amongst the encircling throng. This was far busier than I had experienced in Eisenach. "Watch where you are going, idiots," or, "Keep your eyes open and look where you are going," or "Mind yourselves there," said my father rather irritably, as we were bumped into or our feet trodden upon for the umpteenth time. He was decidedly annoyed by the time he was accidentally struck in the face by a couple of Americans carrying kit bags. "Sorry, Mac" they shouted and were then lost in the general melee around us, before my father could retort. Turning to me he said, "Are you OK, Anni? I have had enough of this. We must seek assistance. I do not know where the hospital lies from here and we cannot keep blundering around in this crowd hoping for inspiration." We fought our way across to an information desk and asked for directions when we finally made it to the centre of the encircling throng.

 It proved to be a long walk from the railway station but at least it was less crowded and a far easier passage to navigate than that which we had experienced in the station forecourt. The main hospital building appeared massive and, as we approached, it rose impressively before us like a gigantic monolith from the past. Indeed, as we walked up the long path to its front entrance, seemingly untouched by the ravages of war, I surmised that it must be the biggest hospital in Leipzig, if not in the whole of Germany. Nurses were going in and coming out, chatting animatedly, laughing and generally behaving as if they were enjoying life to the full. I had not seen such apparent good humour, openly exhibited, in a long time and could not get over the general hustle and verve of the Leipzig community.

 I think both my father and I had palpitations as we entered the foyer. Certainly I was very nervous about meeting my mother again, wondering how ill she really was, and apprehensive as to how she might look. We were directed along a long corridor and stopped in front of a reception desk around which a lot of other people were already milling. Prior to the war, people in Germany would queue in an orderly fashion and await their turn, but since the war this courtesy seemed to have totally disappeared. People were arguing as to who was first, who was second, and who came before whom. It was pandemonium and the exchanges became more heated. Voices were raised but in practice nobody was actually getting anywhere. Dragging me by the hand, my father pushed his way through the vociferous majority until we came to a desk at which sat a very harassed middle-aged lady who was trying to cope on her own with the cacophony of sound assailing her eardrums. She was in a bad-tempered mood and became more irked with every passing minute. It took ages for anyone to get any information from her and, as my father added his voice to all those others surrounding her, she finally decided it was all too much and stomped off. We seemed to be in the hospital for ages and even took to looking hopefully into a number of nearby rooms before we were eventually despatched in the general direction of the relevant ward. We traversed a long corridor, which seemed to be endless in view of the fact that by then we were impatient and eager, so close were we to reaching our goal. We went through a pair of double doors and halted briefly before a single door. We were here at last. My mother should be lying in the room beyond if we had understood our directions correctly. My father shot me a quick reassuring smile, and then slowly pushed open the door. I was right behind him, peering over his shoulder, unmindful of his quiet and cautious entry.

We were confronted by a large bay which contained six beds and, even when we had identified the correct bed, neither of us instantly recognised my mother. She was very pale and thin, and but a shadow of her former self. "Can you see us, Mutti?" I whispered, as we came closer. Her large blue eyes which I so vividly remembered of old, looked even bigger in her shrunken skull, but somehow she seemed to be looking past us rather than at us. This was a surprise to me. She had been told that we were coming and I could not understand her reaction. We hurried to her, hugged her gently and kissed her on her hollow cheeks. She was so frail it was frightening. She then uttered her first words to us and they immediately explained what had been diverting her attention on our arrival. "Where is Jutta?" she asked. My father and I looked at each other and then almost replied in unison. However, I let my father respond uninterrupted. "She has not returned home to us yet, my darling. No doubt she will arrive home soon, but it all takes time you know." Tears welled in her eyes. "Please find her and let me know as soon as you do," she said, as she looked imploringly into our faces and tried to grip my father's sleeve. She became quite agitated and we had to calm her down. We stopped with her for about an hour and a half, but were then advised to leave because the nurse thought our visit was proving too much of a strain for her.

The reunion with my mother had been most moving, if tinged with some sadness that Jutta had not been with us. Tears of happiness streamed down our faces and, as we clung to each other in the final embrace before my father and I departed, she whispered that she was already feeling a lot better for having seen the two of us again. I had never seen my father cry before that moment, but as the double doors closed behind us, he wept as he leaned against the corridor wall outside. I wonder if he thought we would never see her again. I had certainly been shocked at her emaciated and weakened condition.

The hospital was packed with many suffering people not all of whom had beds, and the treatment being provided was of poor quality and very limited, due to there being insufficient staff and inadequate supplies of medication to cater for the vast numbers of patients being brought in. To further compound the situation, some people were dying as a result of being given inappropriate solid food when their stomachs were so unused to nourishment that they could only cope with a light, and sometimes liquid diet. It would be wrong to criticise the staff who were trying to manage under these appalling difficulties and to provide care and support for patients, many of whom it was a considerable wonder that they had survived this long. It was chaotic in the hospital and we resolved, there and then, that, whatever the consequences for my mother, we would all be going home together as soon as it could be arranged. In fact, several weeks were to elapse before the necessary preparations could be finalised for my mother to be allowed to return home with us. We walked back down the long corridor, stepped through the swing doors, turned right and as we stepped out through the front doors, we were assailed by a beautiful blast of fresh air which cleared our lungs of the wretched air which had pervaded the hospital confines. We walked contentedly back to the station hand in hand and with more of a jauntiness in our step. The station forecourt was no easier than when we arrived and we had to fight our way through the crowds to our train. "Just in time," my father yelled above the hubbub, as he pulled me up onto the train. We found a seat, which was most fortuitous given the tardiness of our arrival. Sometimes the German trains which operated in that first year after the cessation of hostilities were so overcrowded that people sat on the floors or wherever else they could find a perch, even on some occasions up on the roof. I recall often seeing people hanging on to the outside of the train's doors and this was the case during our journey home from Leipzig. The doors were slammed shut, the guard whistled for the departure, and we were on our way back to Eisenach. My father was looking far more relaxed than on the outward journey. "The next time we make this journey Anni, your mother is going to be with us," he said confidently. I heartily agreed with him, and we chatted all the way home as we laid plans to give effect to our assertion. We both knew my mother was very weak and ill, but we felt she would be far better at home with us. She had also made it clear, by actions more than words, that she had been very upset at not seeing Jutta with us. I had always felt that Jutta was her favourite and, at the time, took this as further confirmation of my view. I thought she was more concerned at not seeing Jutta than at seeing my father and I. When I look back on that day though, I realise it was a motherly concern for her family as a whole which was her overriding passion rather than a demonstration of favouritism.

When we arrived back in Eisenach, my father decided not to reopen the shop but instead to go straight home with me. He was always fond of cakes and buns, and had been missing my mother's cooking and baking prowess. On the way therefore, by way of a sort of celebration, we bought some cakes and pastry. Arm in arm, laughing and chatting, we walked up the road to our house. "It's been an exhausting, but exciting day, hasn't it Anni?" he said. "It certainly has," I agreed, "but it was lovely to see mum again. Here, let me put the kettle on, Papa, I'll lay the table too. You just sit there." "My," he replied jokingly, "you are going to make someone a wonderful wife, I wish I could have married you too." It was obvious the visit had deeply affected him and he was covering his concern over my mother's condition with jokes. I could see that he was feeling very emotional and I put my arm around him saying reassuringly, "Next week, or soon after, we can fetch her, yes? Then we will be together again and you will not be worried at the large distance which separates us now." My father nodded and seemed grateful for the encouragement and uplifting support, small as it was, that I could offer.

In those days there was no television, no record players, and one either made one's own amusement or listened to the radio. "Would you like to play a game of chess or to try your luck with the cards?" my father asked one day, as the wind and rain beat against the windows discouraging us from venturing forth. "Oh yes, certainly," I replied eagerly. "I would love a game of cards." I hurriedly fetched them from the box of games we kept in the corner of the room and we settled down for some relaxing enjoyment. Sometimes we played for money or sweets. Most times my father would deliberately let me win and yet I thought it was because I was cleverer at the game than he was. The evening usually ended with us having a drink of milk together, but on this particular occasion we finalised our plans for my mother's return. We only hoped that we might have good news for her about Jutta; but no! It was the end of October 1945 when my mother returned to our home with us, but still there was no word as to the fate of my elder sister, Jutta.

Once my mother was back in her own familiar surroundings, although much had changed in the 12 months since we had all departed for Mosbach together, her health slowly picked up and she reckoned she felt better and stronger with every passing day. There was still no news of my sister however, and this was a time of great agonising for both of my parents. Daily, my father, or I, would visit the reception centre seeking news of Jutta but day after day we were greeted with the word "Nothing," and a shake of the head. It got to the stage where we didn't even have to ask the question. We were informed that there were many concentration camps and a few were only just coming to light. The regimes in some had been far more harsh than in others, and the condition of the survivors ranged from very poor to deplorable. It was not possible therefore for the doors of most of the camps just to be opened wide in the expectation that the released inmates would be able to make their own way back into the world. Arrangements for the releases took a long time to sort out, and there were medical conditions to be treated and places to be found where the internees could go and live. Many had faced such trauma during their enforced captivity that it was virtually impossible for them to re-establish their lives without lengthy rehabilitation and counselling. Indeed, in many instances, and as the passage of time was to highlight, the releases from the concentration camps did not bring the instant freedom for which the inmates had for so long yearned. Sometimes years passed before they could shake off the worst of the excesses to which they had been subjected and for many, the scars were to last for the rest of their lives. Displaced persons were asked if they wished to go to America or Israel, and if they so choose, they might be referred to other camps under the protection of the Americans or British while they awaited the necessary clearance and transport. So slow was the processing that the last concentration camp, Fohrenwald, near Wolfratschausen, was not decommissioned until the beginning of 1957.

We believed that my sister had been incarcerated in Lublin camp which was reported not to be as severe as most. Thus, whenever we heard that releases were still being made, we lived in hope that the latest batch of survivors might include my sister, Jutta. Time passed, though, and the trickle of returnees dropped to one or two per week. There were no master lists of whom might have been held where and our hopes of ever seeing her again faded. There was absolutely no news of her fate and we refused to acknowledge the growing evidence that we might not see her again. We lived in perpetual hope that one day she would rejoin us, and we could rebuild our lives together in the happy family unit which had been one of our major strengths in the past.

Chapter 8
The Turning Point, Summer 1945

On 25th April 1945, while the American forces halted their advance at the Elbe and Mulde rivers, the Soviet forces encircled Berlin and were engaged in street to street fighting. Berlin surrendered finally to Soviet Marshal Zhukov on 2nd May 1945, but the principles of partitioning the conquered lands among the victors was already in hand. The Allied conferences of Yalta in February 1945 and Potsdam the following July set the seal on new frontiers and a boundary line, later to become popularly known as the Iron curtain following a speech by Winston Churchill in 1946, was established. The areas to the east of the rivers Elbe and Werra were designated the Russian zone, which was to be controlled by the Soviet Union and thus would follow communist doctrines; while the Americans, British and French occupied the areas to the west where a free democracy prevailed.

Austria became independent of Germany again, although it was not freed of occupying forces, and Vienna was divided into four parts just as was Berlin. While the allies were haggling over the immediate post-war partitioning of the conquered Germany, a massive flow of refugees was flooding into the territory of the Reich, laying to the West of the great Elbe-Werra divide. The vast majority of the population did not wish to live under the control and authority of the Russians and, spurred on by fear in most instances, they fled into the American zone, thereby creating even greater logistical problems for an already decimated region. The Americans were not helped in their endeavours and negotiations by this influx, and their attitude to the future of their vanquished foe was also being greatly influenced by events back in the States.

In America, with his Army virtually at the gates of Berlin and at the hour of perhaps his greatest triumph, President Franklin Roosevelt died quietly. Not only in America but throughout the World, people mourned the passing of this great champion of peace and freedom. And yet, despite all the mourning, there was an underlying feeling of "throwing off the old" and "putting on the new". People wanted to go forward, and not be caught up in setting right problems from the past.

In England, for example, there was a noticeable change of mood which reflected the emergence from a dark and terrible war which had stretched resources to the limit, into the light and freshness of a dawning new era. People were happy again, they could dance in the streets and could relax for the first time in many years. In their victory, there was cause for wild and extravagant celebrations, and for praise of the great leadership qualities of Prime Minister, Winston Churchill. Through his measured oratory and fighting words of wisdom and courage during some of their darkest hours, the people of Britain had been uplifted and strengthened to reach seemingly unassailable heights, and it was not unexpected that they should wish to celebrate their achievements, now that the danger had been conquered. Mingled with the tears of happiness however, were those of sorrow for the many people who would not return, for those who had lost husbands and sons, brothers and sisters, wives and daughters, in the great sacrifice.

There were few who didn't have their own personal experiences of grief. Tens of millions had died in the conflict. The Soviet Union bore the greatest losses with at least 8 million military deaths and more than 7 million civilians. Poland also suffered severely with some of its pre-war population lost – some 6 million people, of whom half were Jews; and Germany, the aggressors, had more than 6 million dead. Nazi Germany, in its Endlosung, or final solution, killed over 6 million Jews, more than half of Europe's pre-war Jewish population. After such slaughter is there any wonder that there was a heartfelt striving for a new and promising beginning. The end of the war in Europe, 8th May 1945, was declared VE (victory in Europe) day by President Harry S. Truman and prime Minister Winston Churchill; but it was very different for those in Germany, especially among the many who were homeless, dispirited and displaced from their original family residences.

By early November 1945, while our family had reclaimed our old house and I had my parents for comfort and support, there was still a feeling of great sorrow and anguish, because the weeks were passing with monotonous regularity and we still had not received any news of my sister, Jutta. Was she alive, or was she dead? Our neighbours were becoming increasingly curious and seemed determined to find out her whereabouts from us. My parents did not wish to be drawn however and kept silent, dismissing their enquiries by telling them that she was staying with friends. After a few weeks of this charade, we started to wonder how long we could continue the pretence, and what would happen if she never did come back. Never came back! It was a thought we did not wish to acknowledge, but as the weeks passed into months and 1945 was replaced by 1946, our doubts really began to surface.

My mother made regular visits to the local commandant's headquarters seeking information, any information, which would ease the burden of our uncertainty, but it was all in vain. She would return home disconsolate time after time, and my parents would then talk and talk into the night. They became more and more disheartened with each passing day. While there were people and refugees arriving in the area we refused to give up hope entirely, even as the steady stream slowed to a trickle during the winter months, and then to one or at the most two per week during the spring of 1946. Not knowing was worse than knowing the truth.

It must have been around seven o'clock one morning in early July when there came a faint knock at our front door. It was an unusual hour for visitors to be calling and we all looked up from our early breakfast. My mother was first out of her chair to answer it and, when she opened the door, momentarily stood transfixed. She could not believe her eyes and, as I peeked around the corner of the lounge door, neither could I. My father, who had stepped out into the hall following closely behind my mother, partly obstructed my view but was the first to react to our caller. There, in the early morning light and illuminated mainly by the yellow glow of the dawn sun from behind such that we couldn't easily see her face, stood a thin and bedraggled Jutta. My sister was back! My mother put her hands up to her mouth while my father pushed past her to almost drag Jutta off the front step and into the dim light spilling from the lounge. Then we were all crying and hugging each other as our emotions engulfed us. A very kindly gentleman who had brought Jutta back to us, stood quietly in the background until the initial warmth and enthusiasm of our welcome was over. He then stepped forward into the light and my mother quickly ushered him indoors along with Jutta who we couldn't release from our arms.

We all talked for a long time and the man eventually departed. We looked around at each other. This was a reunion of which we could never realistically have dreamt. Our prayers had been answered twofold. Our family of four had survived the war, and our house must have been one of the few in Eisenach not to have been bombed or damaged. We had been very, very lucky. Indeed, it was all one big miracle. The following day Jutta and I went round to see my best friend, Edith, and gave her our good news. She was overjoyed for us and later that day we three girls had a little party in her back garden. We had a lot to talk about, catching up on our many months apart, but slowly over the next few weeks, our lives returned to something closely resembling normality. Jutta, who was older than I went to a commercial school where she commenced her training as a secretary.

There was much talk about the withdrawal of the American army, but we did not believe this idle chatter and got down to the task of rebuilding our shattered lives. According to the Potsdam agreement, the area in which we were living had been assigned to the Americans and so we saw no reason to worry. It was one day in late July that the bad news was broken and spread through Eisenach like wildfire. We didn't know why there was a change of heart, but we were informed that the Americans were to leave the town.

It was one of the Americans who had dealt with my situation who came to see and confirmed to us that the American forces were now forced to leave the town. We thought this might just be a rumour, but he came again the next day to say goodbye and assured us that it had already been agreed with the Allies that the whole of Thuringia would fall within the Soviet occupation zone.

From that moment it all happened very quickly – overnight in fact. One evening at the beginning of July the Americans were suddenly up and away, and the very next morning the Russians marched through the gates of Eisenach. Apparently, the Russians had insisted that this little part of Germany was theirs, and to avoid further unnecessary argument the Americans had agreed to withdraw. We felt we had been betrayed.

It was with sinking hearts that we watched one wagon after another wind its way into the town drawn by weary horses and carrying sleepy and drunk Russians. The clatter of tin cans swinging from the sides of the carts could be heard long before the offenders hove into view and, while on the face of it this was just another occupying force, it quickly became clear that our treatment was going to be very different to that which we had experienced whilst under the Americans.

For the second time in just over a year, the German residents were ordered out of their homes and villas so that the occupying soldiers could have the best of the accommodation available; and yet, for some fortunate but no apparent reason, my family were not evicted. There was the ever-present fear however, that the next knock on the door would be a prelude to our enforced departure.

When a Russian family moved out of a residence after such an occupation, the returning occupants were invariably horrified at the state in which their house had been left. Before departing the Russians would urinate everywhere and faeces would be smeared on the walls. The furniture would be gouged or broken, and as much damage as possible would have been inflicted on the property. To some extent we understood their feelings and could not really blame them. When the German soldiers occupied Russian villages during the war, they had been far more cruel, setting fire to the houses, huts and anything else which could provide cover, so that even families with babies found themselves homeless and out in the freezing snow. They therefore came to Germany with vengeance in their hearts and vowed to make East Germany into a concentration camp.

They reduced the amount of available food which had already been in short supply, and we had to survive on smaller and smaller rations. From week to week, and then month to month, matters deteriorated. Every day alterations or new edicts were introduced.

At first the Russian flags were hoisted everywhere as a visible reminder to the populace that the Red Army was in power and from then onwards we must answer to their rule. The electricity was the first utility to be cut off, but then it was closely followed by the gas, and finally the water. Everything was rationed. Every day my mother or father had to queue for one bucket of water. The monthly ration of potatoes was six pounds, and a family of four was expected to live for one month on two ounces of butter and one loaf of bread. It was impossible to survive on such meagre fare, and a flourishing black market developed. If anybody had anything which could be exchanged for food, it was just about possible to obtain sufficient provisions to live reasonably. My mother used to go on her bike to the nearest villages to exchange some of her wares for butter, eggs or even vegetables. One day she was riding through the village when two Russian soldiers stopped her and ordered her to give them her bike. There was nothing my mother could do and she let them have it. I don't know how she got back home, but she was exhausted. At least they didn't take her goods.

My parents sold sugar in our shop as well as sweets, chocolates, coffee and tea, and therefore we had an opportunity to barter on the black market. At first, we were able to exchange sugar for such as butter, but as time went by the supplies to our shop dried up. My mother was then forced into selling several of her gold and diamond rings, her bracelets and her gold chains to keep us all adequately fed.

In time, the plight of the East Germans came to the attention of people abroad, particularly in the USA and Switzerland, and soon thousands and thousands of food parcels were despatched to us, as part of the "Care" parcel project. The distribution arrangements were far from ideal and life became something of a lottery. Planning for the family's future was an impossible dream in such a climate of deprivation and "hand to mouth" survival. Food, and the lack of utilities were not the only privations to which we were subjected. The winter months were the worst, with the severe cold striking easily through to our bodies weakened by lack of adequate sustenance. During the winter of 1946/47 everything was frozen, there was no running water because of blocked or fractured pipes, and toilets were wholly non-functional. Consequently, all the waste had to be taken into the forests and buried under the snow. That in itself was bad enough but when the spring arrived and the warmer weather melted the snow, the stench was overpowering and practically every household was afflicted with diarrhoea and in some cases typhus. Many people died.

Another problem which had to be faced was the shortage of fuel. So that we did not freeze to death during the winter we would go into the woods with small carts to chop down small trees. These would then be transported back to our house where we would cut them up into smaller pieces for burning. It was customary to dry this wood in the attic during the summer season and then store it until it was required. This was obviously a help to the totally inadequate official fuel supplies, but the time came when this enterprise was prohibited by law. For a while after the tree chopping was stopped, we would go into the woods very early in the morning, about 5 o'clock, to avoid other people and any prying eyes, and gather up material for our fire. But soon others learned from our example and it then became too dangerous to venture into the woods at all.

Time passed with a drab repetitiveness, weeks slowly drifted into months, and yet nothing changed, nothing improved. It was a bitter existence not helped by the weather. 1946 bowed out with one of the coldest Decembers that we had known and with the badly depleted stocks of food and fuel, it became a struggle merely to survive. Even so, nobody grumbled or complained because under the Nazis it had been worse. Those horrors were now behind us and the mere thoughts of the past and what might have been, made us feel better. We even managed to celebrate Christmas that year with a nice Christmas tree and a few little presents. Then came the New Year and with it the Russians adopted a higher profile and started to exert their own pressures and terrors upon the civilians in a systematic way.

At first, it would be a few soldiers who might call at the houses and force their way past whoever answered the front door into the living rooms. They would kick the furniture with their boots, barge around throwing their weight about as if daring the occupants to complain and pester any young girls they found there. It seemed that they determined quickly which houses held girls and would return from time to time hoping to catch them alone. Our house did not escape their attention but in the early days they did not find us. They would lurch their way into the house often the worse for drink, damage the furniture or make themselves comfortable with whatever they could find. On a number of occasions my sister and I were in the house hiding, but they did not spot us and would leave with a lot of discordant banging and loud foul-mouthed oaths, sometimes tucking an article or trinket under their arms on the way out.

Our good fortune could not last however, and one day they came back when we were unprepared. They were drunk and laughing, they shrieked and called to each other, and threw their pistols up into the air to frighten us. I was lured into a corner by one of the soldiers who tried to fondle me and interfere with me in a rude and offensive manner. At that moment my mother, who had been working in the kitchen, entered the room to investigate all the noise, which was most fortunate for me. She had always been very courageous and grabbing the shoulder of the brute molesting me, ordered the soldiers from the house. Whether they would have gone became somewhat academic because at that precise instant two of their officers appeared at the door and ordered the men to leave. Surprisingly, the officers also apologised to my mother for the intrusion. It was an experience which left us all shaken. We were conscious that we had been fairly fortunate that day but how long such luck could last, was questionable.

It wasn't long before we found out. I was in the house on my own when I heard a heavy lorry coming down the road. It stopped outside our house and I could hear the crunch of several booted feet upon the path. They were coming nearer but I did not open the door.

From the noises outside they appeared to go around the side of the house into the back garden, and for a while I couldn't hear anything. Then, two of them burst through the door and seized me. They must have broken in somehow, but as they dragged me screaming and struggling to their lorry nobody came to my aid. They threw me into the back and I started to relive the horrors of my earlier journey to Treblinka. They were shrieking and laughing raucously as they drank heavily from bottles of vodka. They forced me to drink the vodka too, very much against my will, but I could not stand up to their manhandling as they poured the liquid down my throat. There were several of them holding onto me as my head was forced back and spilled vodka rolled down my neck wetting my blouse. Hands were groping me. I was horrified at thoughts of what might be about to happen and I was trembling with fear. We had all heard the various stories about girls who were seized from their families and taken on a lorry to Siberia.

We stopped at another house, this time a bit further out into the country. Obviously they had a predetermined itinerary. It was midmorning on a day which was dull, overcast and damp – it was making me feel so very cold, and yet thoughts for my own preservation were still very much to the fore. As the lorry came to a laboured halt all the soldiers jumped off and walked towards the house – they had temporarily forgotten me. This might be my opportunity. There was a lot of shouting and screaming from the house as I turned my attention to the chain across the back of the lorry. I looked to right and left to check that I was not observed and then tried to undo it. Try as I might though, I could not get it unfastened. It was beginning to ease a little when I had to curtail my activities with their return from their forage. They brought with them another screaming and terrified girl of about my age, hauling her across the stony ground and throwing her into the back of the lorry along with me. They climbed in behind her and cracked open some more bottles of vodka. I had lost that chance, but I was determined to be more prepared should a further opportunity present itself. I was watching with a greater awareness of the landscape through which we were passing. I did not recognise our surroundings and did not know how far I was from home. As we bumped along with our gaolers becoming more drunk and more attentive to us two girls with every passing mile, I wondered – O God, for how much longer?

We turned into a lane straggled on each side by an assortment of trees and through my slightly obscured vision, I could see a stream of old houses set back in their own grounds. My female companion was very frightened and was sobbing to herself. I wanted to converse with her and at least whisper that she should be ready to jump off the lorry when I nudged her. I certainly had no intention of leaving her alone with our kidnappers, but she was becoming hysterical whether through fear, drink or a combination of the two, and I was unable to communicate with her.

The lorry pulled up in front of some rather grand gates, but this time they left one of their number with us. He was rather the worse for drink fortunately, and I was convinced this was as good a time as any to try to make a break for it. As he turned away from us to watch his retreating buddies, I fumbled with the chain and all at once it fell free in my hands. I jumped down from the back dragging my young companion with me. We ran as fast as we could away from the scene, making as much use as we could of any natural cover which might hide us from any pursuers. Our guard set off in pursuit but had hardly travelled 20 yards when he fell over, presumably unsteady from the liquor, and seemed to lose interest in following us any further.

Eventually, when we felt we could run no further, we knocked as loudly as possible on a nearby house. The door was answered by two very kind people to whom we explained our predicament. They took us in and we stayed with them until dusk. No doubt the Russians were looking for us, but they did not come to the house and after a little while we became more relaxed. Once darkness fell these people took us home to our parents in their little car. They dropped the younger girl off first, and after that they took me home. When I arrived my parents were glad to see me again, but shocked since it was so late by now. My parents had been because they had no idea what had happened and had returned home from the shop to find a busted rear door and signs of a struggle in the living room.

Once they were over their joy at my safe return and we had had time to reflect, it was abundantly clear to us all that something had to be done – and as a matter of urgency. We were under no illusions that the Russians would probably come back and next time we were unlikely to be so fortunate. I had to be hidden in the house where I would not be found. We had a little sewing room which led off the dining room and the door to this was already wallpapered so that it could not be easily distinguished from the surrounding wall area. The soldiers invariably called in mid-morning when they came, so every day after breakfast, my mother would hide me in there and push a wardrobe across the front of the closed door. I spent many hours locked within with no view on the outside world, thinking, writing and dreaming of happier times. It was almost like the Stanislaws' cellar revisited. This situation was ridiculous, however. Here I was a prisoner in our own home, not allowed out even after dark. We could not keep this up for ever and we started contemplating our escape to the West.

Chapter 9
Decision Time

Eisenach before the War had been a haven of peace to which we had fled in 1938 with high hopes for the future. My mother's Jewish origin and the growing persecution of such people in Kołobrzeg had forced us to rethink our lives and we had come to Eisenach where absolutely nobody knew us or of our family history. My parents thought that we would be safer there than on the Baltic, even though it meant giving up so much of what they had established over the years; and they'd picked this little town because it was renowned for its natural beauty, its abundance of flora and fauna, and for its rivers, forests and mountains. It had been an idyllic spot with a healthy climate and it held countless happy memories for us all. In the summer we used to enjoy trips into the surrounding country, swimming in the lakes, and sledging, skiing and skating during the winter. It was a place where I had grown up through my early teens in a contented family atmosphere, playing games most evenings and listening to my father play the piano. He was an accomplished pianist, indeed many thought brilliant, and had played in concerts before huge audiences. Eisenach had been a place of great naturalness which had provided many great men with the necessary inspiration to execute great works. Such personages as the great poet, Wolfgang von Goethe, had lived there, sharing his time between Eisenach and Weimar; but conditions which were now being imposed by the Russians meant that all we had come to treasure were but memories and that any future must lie elsewhere. Eisenach had lost its innocence and its tranquillity.

It was time to move on. Yet again we were being forced to uproot our family in circumstances totally beyond our control. There was considerable sadness at the prospect and I fell to reminiscing about my adopted home town. Eisenach is situated in the western part of Thuringen, and its past is closely interwoven with the fortunes and misfortunes of its famous castle, the "Wartburg". The castle was constructed in 1067 and at the beginning of the 19th Century was recognised as a national sanctuary. Famous are the stories about Saint Elisabeth, about Martin Luther who translated the New Testament from Greek into German, and about Richard Wagner, the composer, who wrote the "Tannhauser" there in 1862. I suppose the most famous claim to fame is, however, the Bach house and the associated monument. I used to pass by these on my way to school and had not appreciated at the time why the Church music he composed should evoke such emotions and interest that regularly thousands of people would choose to make pilgrimages to view his old house. It was actually very small and to my eye very insignificant. One can only surmise at the effects which all that hammering of visitors' feet on the warped and creaking floorboards can have had on the structure. Every year on the anniversary of his birthday, 21st March 1700, thousands would arrive to celebrate the event with music and candlelight.

Like so many things, the War had put an end to all that. The Bach house and the Luther House were both severely damaged during the War. Although they would be rebuilt sometime in the future, the Russian government was not very sympathetic to the preservation of our heritage and many artefacts, etc. were lost. The lack of plentiful building materials was, and always has been, a ready excuse for postponing rebuilding programmes. What a state my native homeland was in.

My reverie and reminiscences were interrupted by the opening of the door to my temporary hideaway in the sewing room. I stepped out to join our parents in the living room. The plight of my sister and I in the current situation was discussed at great length, and it was abundantly clear that our circumstances were unlikely to improve in the foreseeable future. Shut away in the sewing room for most of the daylight hours was blighting and totally disrupting our lives. As time passed and the visits to our house by the Russians became less frequent we started to become more venturesome, but we still had to be careful. Even without their intrusion, though, the subsistence level of existence which the Russian system imposed did not allow the sort of life we wished to lead. We concluded that the family's best chance of a viable and happy life rested upon our flight to the West zone, and over the next few weeks we started to lay tentative plans.

The first step was for my father to sell his business, a move which he quickly achieved in the early Autumn of 1947, a young lady purchasing both the property and the stock. He then went into partnership with a businessman who was already having great success in the small-tool trade. This proved to be a good financial step initially, but conditions rapidly deteriorated in the DDR and, when the authorities banned all trading with the West BRD in 1948, it became impossible for my parents to earn enough money. My parents became extremely worried about the future. We had often spoken of moving to the West but it was not that easy despite the fact that my father had loosened his ties in the business community. 1947 had passed all too quickly and, once the early euphoria at the cessation of hostilities had worn off, the population had sunk into a tedium and depression brought about by the conditions under which they were forced to eke out their existence. The New Year 1948 was heralded in with the customary peeling of bells, but there were few celebrations and the people's morale was at a very low ebb. An associate of my father's who was a close neighbour, Fritz Klueger, offered to take me across the border and I got quite excited as I packed my few belongings for the trip. "It's quite easy", he said, "if you know how! As a matter of fact I am going across next week. Everything has been arranged and I would be quite happy to take Anneliese." Arranged? Easy? How? We were somewhat incredulous. He laughed heartily. "The police. The police are helping me to cross safely to the West." We didn't believe him. Perhaps this was black market talk and such escapes had been noteworthy for going wrong. After careful consideration, my parents withdrew their permission for me to go at the last minute, believing more care needed to be taken in the planning and execution of our flight. The following week we saw Fritz load his luggage into a car and drive off in the convoy of East German police on motorbikes. "There he goes", said my father. "He was not joking after all!"

The summer came and went and I became more and more unhappy. My sister was employed at that time in an office on the outskirts of town and while she enjoyed her job, her desire to flee to the West was steadily growing, along with mine. Our family could not put matters off indefinitely. We needed to adopt a definite plan but we seemed unable to come up with any really promising ideas. We could cut loose from the tool business fairly easily but our house and furniture were a different proposition. We had to find a buyer for the house and we would have to put forward a sound reasoned argument for selling up if we were to avoid deep trouble from the East German police. At the same time, any other preparations would have to be performed as discreetly as possible so as not to draw attention to ourselves.

My parents planned everything very carefully. Firstly, they set about selling some of our furniture in dribs and drabs, taking care to leave sufficient around to suggest the house was still furnished and occupied. They then sold the house quietly to a trustworthy neighbour and friend who was both understanding of and sympathetic towards our position. My father was meticulous in his approach but time was of the essence and I am sure he sold at lower prices than we might have done if we had not been so desperate to depart. Once we had arrived at this state of affairs we were in a position where we could depart at very short notice and it was merely a case of deciding who should go first.

We could not all leave together because this would have looked too suspicious to the ever-alert Russian-German police. I had become very impatient however and for the last few weeks had been chomping at the bit eager to go. I had been in touch with one of my father's business colleagues and pleaded with him to take me across to the West next time he was going. He had readily agreed to my entreaties and I approached my father to see if he would allow me to seize this opportunity. After some discussion, it was decided that I should be the first in the family to depart, but they refused to allow me to go with the businessman. As an alternative, my parents contacted some people with a lorry whom they knew also wished to cross the border. A few pieces of our furniture were to be squeezed onto the vehicle and the departure date of 5th October 1948 was agreed.

As this date approached, I made an especial effort to visit some of my best friends, and Edith in particular. When I told her about my imminent departure, she was heartbroken. I attempted to persuade her to join me in my emigration but she was too scared and opined that the intolerance of and persecution by the Russian regime could not last forever. She was not to be dissuaded from that view and long were our embraces, chatter, laughter and tears, in the prelude to our final waves of goodbye. It was at such times that I found myself most likely to question the validity of my own convictions, but there was no going back now – my future lay somewhere to the West, where I was sure I would make new friends. My old friends however, would remain forever treasures within my store of memories. I also had a boyfriend whom I had known for approximately two years, and his love, kindness and understanding had helped me many times during the dark and dismal months of the early occupation. When I gave him my news he was so shocked he cried a lot and tried to talk me out of it. It was very hard for me, but I was not ready for marriage, or even a firm commitment, at that stage of my life. I had grand dreams of seeing the World and a desire to start life afresh unbesmirched by the trials and tribulations of the last ten years. We embraced and our tears mingled as we said our last fond farewells. I had to tear myself away from him and he took me home in virtual silence. I never saw him again.

Chapter 10
Farewell to the East

The 5th October I saw as the answer to my prayers and, while it signalled the start of another separation from my parents, it was also the start of a new beginning on which I was pinning all my hopes. It was early in the morning, around four o'clock, that the heavily laden lorry rolled complainingly up to the front of the house and stopped, amidst a swirl of dust and dark exhaust. Out stepped Frau Kuehne and her husband into the deserted street and made their way to our front door as quietly as they could, their feet scrunching on the gravel beneath.

"Well, Anni. Are you ready for the great day?", Frau Kuehne asked as she and her husband were ushered into the hallway where we were all standing awaiting them. "Yes", I replied. I had been prepared for some time and my few belongings which I was taking with me were already stacked by the front door. Herr Kuehne took these out to the lorry and after struggling for some time, managed to find space into which to pack them while I turned towards my parents. It was time to say my farewells. This was the hardest part of the whole exercise because we did not know when, or if, we would see each other again. The fragmentation of our family previously had been enforced upon us and we had had no option. This time it was a voluntary decision which was leading to our separation and, while it comes to most families when their children elect to leave the bosom of the family home, we were to be separated by a barrier of cultures it would be difficult to breach. I found it particularly hard to part with my family, but it was a decision we had all reached collectively and we knew it was in all our best interests. I was nineteen and my future lay out there in the "bright lights" off to the West.

My mother and father, and also Jutta, queued up to embrace me with tears welling in their eyes. "Anni, don't forget what I told you yesterday, will you now?" said my mother as she wrapped me tenderly in her arms. We had talked long into the previous night and I will always cherish those last conspiratorial hours as treasured moments when we were together for the last time as a close-knit family. "Goodbye Mutti, Goodbye Papa, Goodbye Jutta," I called as I gave them one last hug and ran out to the lorry. I jumped into the front seat next to Frau Kuehne and looked back at my mother, my father and my sister as Herr Kuehne noisily engaged the gears and the lorry moved off, slowly gathering pace just as the sun was rising hazily behind us. I waved and waved, and as we gathered speed I was suddenly struck by the realisation that I was somehow on my own. No longer had I the protection afforded by my parents. All children eventually reach the stage when they decide it is time that they left the family nest and branch out on their own. I suppose that they will have similar feelings to those I was experiencing at that moment but if I had had the choice I would have preferred to stay with my family and friends. As it was, the lack of opportunity and the harshness of the Communist regime meant my future had more promise in the green pastures to the West.

I kept watching my family through tear filled eyes until they were there no more, and as the dust swirled around the drumming wheels, I gazed vacantly out of the window not seeing the unfolding landscape but merely their faces and the vivid memories of our lives together. Herr Kuehne drove rather fast, and was tense and more than a little nervous in case we were stopped. Also on board was, Fritz, the Kuehnes' son.

As the miles unfolded without mishap however, he began to relax and to talk about a multitude of things – what it was like in the big cities and what we could expect. He gave me lots of advice and we were all happy, laughing and singing, as we pondered the joys and freedoms we would soon be experiencing. We were all aware that our past was now behind us and that we had to look to the future. We had to start almost from scratch with only what we had on the lorry, but after what had gone before we could only imagine that our fortunes were on the way up. I still harboured mixed feelings about the upheaval and having to leave my parents behind, but I was carried along in the general euphoria.

We had soon left Eisenach behind us and travelled via Berka towards Dippach and the border. Dusk was fast approaching as we drove into the outer suburbs of Dippach and we were constantly being reminded that we were not out of danger yet. Indeed, if anything, our journey was becoming more hazardous. The Russians were guarding a number of places but they were well hidden and we only became aware of their presence when we heard shooting. Generally, it was not in our direction and for that we were thankful. When we rounded another bend in the road however we realised our turn was about to come. Somewhat to our amazement and dismay we saw two armed Russian soldiers manning a barrier away in the distance. We frantically threw glances to left and right in search of a road or reason to leave our present route.

There was nowhere for us to turn off however and we approached with mounting apprehension and fear, drawn forward inexorably as if on a rope towards our fate. The soldiers slowly swung their guns off their shoulders and pointed them vaguely in our direction as Herr Kuehne slowed the lorry as if he was about to stop – and indeed I thought that he was. Suddenly though, Herr Kuehne shouted to us to hold tight and hit the accelerator with his foot. The lorry crashed through the barrier amid much shouting from the soldiers. They started shooting. I was sure we were going to be hit but everything was happening so fast there was no time in which to process such thoughts. It was very noisy with the screams from our over-revving engine, the splintering and shattering of the barrier, the shouting and shooting from the soldiers, and the rumbles, creaks and sounds of breaking glass from the furniture in the rear of the lorry. I began to wonder why we had bothered to waste our time and effort bringing this furniture with us because it was a dead give-away. Still, we were through.

One hurdle down – but how many more yet to be overcome? On our arrival in Dippach, we parked the lorry in a little lane someway short of the centre of town and walked the rest of the way. The Kuehne's took me to a family who had organised an Identity Card for me – it did not contain a photograph but it was not until later that this became necessary. The important point was that I had to adopt a new identity very quickly and remember my new name, address, and time and date of birth, even as we were moving on.

We walked to the station where Frau Kuehne said her goodbyes. I was to travel on from here with Fritz to look after me, and if all went well and without a hitch, when I alighted from the train for which we were then waiting I would be in the Rheinland. All of this had been prearranged by my parents and we had rehearsed it until I knew it all by heart. Once in the West, I had to make my way to the town of Hilden where I would contact Frau and Herr Breuer. It all seemed so simple and I had their address secreted in my bag. I thought I was to all intents as good as there, but little did I realise that if things could go wrong, they would.

We stood back in the shadows and watched as the train drew into the platform and, as it came to a halt, we joined the mad dash forward towards the doors. While we were caught up in the general melee of the heaving throng, a German-Russian policeman strolled slowly but purposefully towards us. "Halt! You two with the cases," he directed in our direction. "where do you think you are going? And why have you so much luggage with you?" He grabbed Fritz's shoulder and gesticulated towards me. "Young lady, why are you wearing two suits?" I turned to find his eyes boring into mine thereby making me all the more nervous. "Identity cards," he grunted. I fumbled in my bag and as I passed mine to him I responded to his enquiry in trembling voice. "I want to catch the train to the Rhineland. Please don't make me miss it."

I hadn't thought at the time when I'd dressed earlier that morning that the extra bulk of my clothing would be noticed but now, in hindsight and upon reflection, it was clearly my fault our cover had been blown. It's easier, much easier, to be wise after the event but I had not foreseen that by trying to wear and carry too many of my personal effects, I would be jeopardising the whole venture. I started sweating. "Name? Date of birth?" barked my inquisitor. I had forgotten my date of birth. My only hope now was to pretend that I was mentally deficient. It didn't work. Fritz became really annoyed and harangued me for my foolhardiness. We were not allowed to get on the train but had to watch despairingly as it drew out of the station. My spirits sank. We were instructed to follow closely behind the officer who had waylaid us and who, by now, was looking very pleased with himself. We were conducted into a waiting room where there were a lot of other people who had obviously made the same mistake as ourselves, burdening themselves down with tell-tale impedimenta. I was searched and my luggage was inspected meticulously item by item. I was then questioned by a second policeman and when he asked me details of my identity I still could not remember most of it and had to continue with the pretence that I was mentally deficient. They kept on at me, and my interrogation persisted for some considerable time. However, when they learned that I was also unable to sign the signature of my new name as it was shown on my Identity Card, they realised my documents were forged and the game was up.

Fritz Kuehne was becoming more furious by the minute but he, along with everybody else in that waiting room, was eventually bundled into a battered old lorry and transported to Rothenburg. It was one of those nice autumn days with a blue and sunny sky streaked with slim tentacles of wispy cirrus; and yet a tinge of cold carried in a swirling wind, forewarned of the winter to come. The trees were shedding their leaves which had taken on a myriad of beautiful shades of red, brown, orange, lemon and green. As we passed they would dance and twirl along the road in a farewell performance to a long hot summer. Our journey was a long one and, as it unfolded, I slowly became more uncomfortable, ill, tired and frightened. The sun was low in the sky, casting ominous shadows as we pulled up in front of a large imposing prison in Rothenburg, and were ordered to alight. Harsh voices assailed us from all directions and we were all somewhat bewildered by our sudden downturn in circumstances. Like criminals, we were shunted and shoved around as we entered through the grim portals of the forbidding grey edifice silhouetted before us.

We were conducted into a large waiting area and were segregated into separate groups of men and women. We were all very hungry but that had to wait while we were "processed". There were so many people crammed into the room this took some time, an exercise not helped by the lack of any apparent order. There were young and old, and single women with children who just could not cope with the situation. I felt very sorry for them. We were given a register in which we all had to sign our names. It was a massive book and I could not believe that so many people had tried to escape and had passed this way before me. I was deeply shocked and distressed when I saw the signature of my parents in this book. I had not known what had happened to them since my departure from Eisenach, whether they had been sent back or if they had continued their journey. Sight of their name in the register had only compounded my anxiety.

After signing the register I made myself as comfortable as I could on the floor and awaited developments. It was at least an hour later before a German policeman entered the room and handed out some food. This consisted of a raw herring, a stale crust of bread and a tin mug of cold fresh water but we were all so ravenous that we were just grateful for something to eat.

After this stomach-turning repast, a policewoman who gave the impression that she was important, took several people to their sleeping quarters. I was shocked when I was shown into what looked to me like a prison cell. As the door clanged behind me, I was plunged into a clammy unrelenting darkness. I hadn't expected a nice soft mattress with a warming quilt but I was not wholly prepared for the bed to which I tentatively groped my way. My fingers touched rough wooden planking, and then a crumpled damp blanket. I lay down on this bench which was covered with straw and wrapped the rough smelly blanket around me. Strands of straw were sticking into me and I was feeling somewhat woeful and unloved. So much for my bright new beginning.

Suddenly, out of the darkness, came a young woman's gruff voice. Was I scared! I had thought that I was alone in my dark retreat. She sounded common, threatening and made a number of rude and offensive remarks. She raucously enquired about the goodies she hoped I had brought with me and whether I had any valuables, but I chose not to answer. During the night however, I heard her get up and rummage amongst my luggage. I was sure that she wanted to steal from me and I found myself sleeping only very fitfully as I tried to keep an ear open for my unwelcome companion. What I might do I had not really considered. Besides, I was also shivering with cold and my stomach was grumbling and complaining over the lack of proper food. The night seemed to drag on interminably, and I was very glad when morning came. I'd hardly slept at all and felt no better than when I retired.

As the first tinges of a cold grey dawn lightened the small high window in my little prison, the heavy door was swung open and my unsavoury companion and I were led back towards the main hall. As we walked along, I sneaked my first real look at my night-time partner and noted her unkempt appearance and general demeanour were just as intimidating as her voice. I was feeling especially thankful therefore to be out of our cell unscathed and to be rejoining all the other internees where I resolved to keep well away from her. By the time we arrived in the large reception area, most of the others were already milling around in there, disgruntled and deprecatory, loudly expressing their discontent. I cannot say their vociferous mouthings-off appeared to get them anywhere, however. I was more concerned about my hunger pangs and the need for some sustenance – any sustenance.

Breakfast. The thought conjured up mouth-watering visions in my mind's eye. I wonder if there will be hot coffee and some rolls this morning. One can dream but I suppose it was only wishful thinking. Eventually a man walked into the hall where we were all seated, expectantly waiting. He was carrying a large box of raw herrings which he threw literally across the floor and for which we had to make a hasty grab. Then followed crusts of bread and finally, some cold water which didn't even look clean, was dispensed into tin mugs that were unwashed from the previous night. We were all starving and fell to eating with relish although the greasy oil of the fish and the flaking scales were off-putting to say the least.

On this second day we were questioned individually by members of the American forces. I was ushered into a small room which housed a large desk with sheaves of important papers laying upon it and through which one or other of my interrogators would periodically thumb. A senior American officer sat centrally behind this desk conducting the interview, flanked on either side by two other officers who looked totally bored with the whole proceedings. Over in one corner was yet another American with a few stripes on his sleeve, who was accompanied by the translator. I was asked dozens of questions like: How did I cross the border? Where did I obtain my forged passport? With only a very limited knowledge of English, I tried to explain to them what was going on in the Russian sector and how life was unbearable under that cruel regime, but they just did not understand. How could they? And the translator was no help. I pleaded not to be sent back to the East Zone, but it soon became clear that I had no chance of succeeding. I was told that I would be detained there for a few more days and would then be returned across the border.

We had to stay in Rothenburg for three nights and, on the last evening, I pleaded with one of the American soldiers guarding us to let me go. He refused. We were in a sort of no-man's land and could see the West zone from our prison. So near and yet so far. It would have been such a simple walk into the next village. One lady sold her wedding ring in order to buy her freedom and to purchase food. I had nothing to sell. I had not come so far however, only to be thwarted at the final hurdle. A small group of American soldiers, off duty, bored, eating chewing gum, kicking stones on the ground, making jokes, smoking, and laughing amongst themselves, was at one point all that stood between me and my freedom. Here was my chance, or so I thought. I was hidden from all but this little group. I needed no transport and could walk quickly and quietly to the village which lay off in the distance. I stepped out into the open and strode purposefully down the road before me. Maybe they did not understand my response in fragmented English when they challenged me. How could they? Anyway, they presumably had their orders even when off duty. They refused to let me pass and I was reluctantly forced to rejoin my fellow captives.

Fritz Kuehne came up to me, smiling pleasantly and enquiring what I had been doing with myself. What did he think I had been up to. There wasn't much to do in this God-forsaken hole. I shrugged my shoulders and walked away. He was annoyed and so was I. I thought he should have looked after me better than he had. In hindsight, perhaps I was being unfair to him and it wasn't really his fault, but at the time I was fuming with the disappointment that I should be so close to escape and yet could not pull it off. On the third day of our stay at Rothenburg, we were informed that the train taking us back to the Russian sector would arrive early the next morning and we should be prepared to leave at first light.

Chapter 11
My Return to the East

It was the 9th October when I collected up my few belongings for the return journey to Eisenach. Everything had been in vain, and I was feeling wretched. The tiring long crossing from East to West, all the careful and detailed planning by my parents and others, all of this had ended in abject failure. The train arrived at 4 o'clock in the morning and as we huddled together on the desolate platform, some of the people were undecided about boarding the train, discussing the feasibility of escape and whether the risk was worth taking. To me, such a venture appeared foolhardy in the extreme because already there were armed German-Russian police on the platform waiting to board with us and some dogs with their handlers patrolling in the vicinity. Two German men came up to me and suggested that we should get onto the train but just as it was setting off, we should open the door on the far side and jump off. My courage deserted me on this occasion, and while others did resort to this action, I stayed secure in my carriage and do not know what happened to them once they had leapt clear.

Within minutes of leaving the train was in the East and our guards alighted before the train sped deeper into East Germany. I was very tired and in spite of feeling very cold and hungry, I soon fell asleep in my seat. A very kind nun sitting opposite me tried to figure out where I was going and from where I was coming. She was only trying to be friendly but I kept the conversation fairly brief as I flitted in and out of a semi-conscious state. Fritz Kuehne alighted from the train some way before my journey's end and the carriage was deserted except for the nun and I. I was thus alone for the latter stages of the ride, and was immensely thankful when she awoke me as Eisenach station hove into view. If it hadn't been for her I think I would have passed through my alighting point totally oblivious of my familiar surroundings. The train ground to a halt with much screeching from its wheels and brakes, and amid clouds of billowing smoke, almost as if it too was utterly exhausted and tired of carrying on.

I climbed down wearily from the carriage clutching my luggage close to me but all the while observing what was transpiring about me. I chose not to follow the majority of my fellow travellers who made their way into the waiting room to deliberate on their next move. I decided instead to visit the station restaurant, and sat down. I didn't know what my next step would be and where to go.

A gentleman who sat some distance from me and was obviously watching me, came over to my table and asked if I wanted to eat anything or if I would like a beer. I accepted because I was very hungry and thirsty. He tried to make conversation, but I was too scared and did not trust anybody.

I thanked him and as I was just about to get up, a German policeman followed by a Russian soldier marched through the door. I was terrified and clung to this gentleman, who covered me up with his coat to protect me. I was very grateful to him, and he wanted me to come with him, but I said, "I am sorry, but I am going to visit a friend." More people entered the restaurant and while it was busy I walked briskly out of the station with a measured tread and to give the impression that this was something I did regularly.

It was early morning and the street was deserted, except for a Russian soldier with a rifle over his shoulder, who tried to follow me. I ran off, as quick as I could. I knew that by now my parents and my sister would have left Eisenach so there was no point in returning to our old house. After twenty minutes, I finally arrived at the hotel where my friend Edith lived. I looked around me nervously, but I did not see anybody – the streets were deserted since it was very early in the morning. I knocked at the wooden door and hoped somebody would answer. I waited again, then knocked louder in case they had not heard me, but it was in vain. I suppose I could return later, I thought.

An idea came to me to go and see Herr Maedler and his wife. I should have thought of this before, as the Maedlers were friends of my parents who used to visit us frequently, and they lived not far from the station. I walked on with new hope and confidence, but as I was crossing the road I was stopped all of a sudden by a *volkspolizei* who asked where I was going. I didn't tell him about the Maedlers, instead I said, "I have been to visit my friend, but she is not answering the door yet, so I will have a drink somewhere and go back later."

The policeman didn't believe me and said, "You better come with me to the station."

"Why? I haven't done anything wrong – I am not coming with you!" and I tried to run away, but he ran after me, got hold of me and dragged me into a nearby car.

"You can tell the commandant your story," and off he drove at some speed, until we arrived at the station.

"Come with me and don't argue, I'll take you to the commandant who will deal with you." And with a smirk on his face, he ushered me into a big office where a big well-fed man with a moustache sat behind a desk which had seen better days. The walls were plastered with pictures of prominent men in uniform and of course Josef Stalin who had the largest painting.

"Well, Fraulein, what were you doing at this hour in the street, and why are you wearing lots of clothes?" I explained the clothes were for my friend, and since I was not able to carry them, I put them on.

"Nonsense!" He shouted, "I don't believe you, and now I want to see your identity card."

"All right," I said, and fumbled in my bag, pretending it was in there.

"Where is it then, Fraulein?" and he banged his fist on the desk, all the time looking at me with his beady and suspicious eyes.

"I can't find it, Herr Commandant, I must have lost it."

"What's your name, anyway, and date of birth?"

Now I had to make up my name and said, "Maria Keller." Then he rang a bell and a man in uniform appeared. He shouted again: "Take this girl downstairs for further interview." The man took me downstairs into a dark room and closed the door. I was terrified and had to think if I could invent another story.

I had another idea. Soon one of his mates walked in.

"You will be punished if you have no identity card with you."

"What sort of punishment?"

"You will see, Fraulein, but first you must give me more information about yourself."

"I have told the Commandant everything already, and I am innocent."

He wouldn't listen. "All nonsense," he said.

I was really scared but tried out my new idea.

"I will tell you. You need to know that I am a Communist and I try to find people who are against our regime. Mostly I find them lurking about in or around the station. I give you my word that I can help to find such scoundrels."

"I see," he said. "Still, we would like to see your identity card."

"I know. I told you, I lost it and I was on my way to find it. As soon as I find it, I will come back here. I have lived here many years and I am very fond of the DDR."

He listened and said to me: "Fraulein, wait here, I am going to tell the Commandant your story."

Now I was frightened, but I hoped they would believe me. I sat there for an hour. I heard nothing but the clock ticking. Then I heard footsteps. They came nearer. My heart was pounding and I started to pray, "Please, dear God, help me, and forgive me for having told lies." Then the door opened and the man beckoned me to come with him to the Commandant.

"Ah, Fraulein, good to see you again. I have heard you are one of us. Great; nice to have met you, Comrade Maria. We look forward to seeing you again. Great news that you will help us. We like people like that. You can go now, back to your friend and I hope she will welcome you. Please come and visit us as soon as you can, and we hope you can find some of those villains who try to get over the border. We Communists must always be like a family, and we thank you. I hope you will find that card soon, or that somebody will forge it."

"I will do my best, Commandant, and come to see you very soon."

"Thanks, Comrade Maria, all the best now."

He got up kissed me on both cheeks, opened the door and waved me off with a broad smile. I was relieved.

I walked away, thanked God for his help, turned a corner and started to run towards the house where I remembered the Maedlers lived, and I hoped they still lived there. I found the house, rang the bell and waited.

I felt awful for awakening these family friends so early in the morning but I could hear footsteps coming down the road and I played entreatingly on the doorbell with greater urgency.

After a while Frau Maedler opened the window to see who it was, and when she saw me she came running downstairs and opened the heavy front door and let me in.

"Come on in Anni! Be quick," she whispered, as she hurriedly pulled me inside and closed the door before the footsteps outside came too close.

We climbed three flights of stairs and eventually entered her flat. Now and again she stopped, being out of breath. Once she asked "What has happened to you?" but realised that she was better conserving her breathing until we were upstairs. She would look at me, shake her head and then continue laboriously up a few more steps. Eventually we entered her flat where her husband was preparing to go to work and I was certainly relieved to be able to put down my luggage.

Herr Maedler was pleased to see me and begged me to tell them the whole story.

Frau Maedler looked after me like a mother. She was an excellent cook and a loving wife. They gave me a good meal and a bed. I told them my story and they informed me that they themselves were no longer safe. Herr Maedler was an engineer and the Russians were looking for people such as he, with skills and experience, to bolster their own economy. The Maedlers could not afford to be caught with me in their house and I might be discovered by virtue of being in their house. It was a volatile situation and I could not stay there longer than was absolutely essential because my presence would be inevitably endangering all of us.

I stayed with them for only the one night revelling in the plush warm bed to which I had been directed. It was the first time I'd slept soundly since leaving my parents and having gorged myself on the excellent food with which my hosts had so willingly plied me. Things were already moving very quickly; in the morning Herr Maedler told me he would take me in his van to get as near as he could to a family whom the Maedlers knew, who would help me

En route to Berka, he explained that he had friends living not far from the spot where he would deposit me. He explained to me in some detail the route which I should follow through a thick pine tree forest.

"This is as far as I can take you, Anni. Be careful, and I wish you all the best of luck. We would both like to hear from you maybe one day." The Maedlers had been very close friends of my parents and Herr Maedler was very concerned for my well-being. He wished me luck and hugged me.

Then he was gone. That was the last time I ever saw him, although I later learned that he and his family managed to sell their beautiful house and fled the area.

It was dark and so foggy that I could hardly see my hand in front of me and I was very frightened. It was still early in the morning and I had to plunge into a tall, dark wall of conifers. To walk through a thick pine tree forest would have been disconcerting at the best of times but with the fog closed in around me, water dripping from overhanging branches and the clammy tendrils reaching out of the nothingness through which I was groping, only added to my feelings of disorientation and isolation in a strange environment. The pine needles scrunching under my feet provided the only sound I could hear and that was muffled eerily by the enshrouding fog. I was more frightened than I'd been for some time. I love pine trees when the sun is glinting tantalisingly through their dense foliage but they were so thickly clumped in places that anybody could have been hiding in there and I would have been none the wiser until I touched them. I might be hidden from my would-be captors but how was I to know if I was going in the right direction? There was no way of telling. If only there had been a moon for me to follow.

It became a little lighter with the passage of time but I was still scared. Now and again I would hear a rustling in the trees and my heart would pound as I thought it was somebody. I wished that I had not taken so much luggage, but this was all I had in the World and I treasured much of it. I really came to regret not having heeded earlier advice and my previous experiences not to look to over laden, but having come this far I was not minded to abandon any of it in the middle of these woods. I must have struggled blindly on for over an hour before the fog slowly began to lift and I could see a house looming up before me. It was one house alone as I had been told to expect, and as I surveyed it, I thought it looked more like a farmhouse than anything else. I began to feel happier now that I had found some form of habitation – I certainly did not feel so lonely but then neither did I have the confidence to be sure that this was indeed the house I sought.

I walked somewhat hesitantly towards it and as I walked up the path I was able to ascertain that the number of the house was indeed the one which I had been told to find. I stood there awhile not wishing to awaken these good people so early in the morning, and was so tired that I leant against the wall and stared vacantly into space, until all of a sudden, I heard footsteps and movement within the house. I decided then to take the plunge and ring their bell.

There was no immediate response and the sounds within ceased. In case the bell was not working then knocked at the well-weathered woodwork a number of times but several minutes must have elapsed before the door slowly moved back on its hinges and I could just discern a gentleman's face peering through the narrow slit.

"Who is it?" I heard a man's voice.

"It's me, Anni, Herr Maedler has sent me to you."

Again I waited, then the door was opened by a gentleman in a dressing gown. "Oh Anni, come in!" He introduced me to his wife and daughter and welcomed me. I was relieved, but did not know what to expect next.

"Come in, Anni, and sit down, you look so tired."

"Herr Maedler told me your name, it is Gustav Mueller, I believe?"

"Yes, that's right, call me Gustav and my wife's name is Erika."

"Hello Anni," she shouted from the kitchen, "and not to forget my lovely daughter Susanne, we call her Susie, and her boyfriend."

As he ushered me into his cold but dry home, I apologised to him for awakening his family so early and explained to him and his wife who had meanwhile joined him, who I was and how I came to be there. After such simple introductions they made me welcome and his wife rapidly rustled up some food. Even as I ate a most satisfying breakfast, plans were being laid for my flight into the West Zone. They were very friendly people and made me very comfortable. I was offered a change out of my wet clothes and was soon seated before a roaring fire in one of their daughter's dresses while my clothes dried on a nearby airer. I stayed with them throughout that day and through the bulk of the following night.

Their daughter was very attractive and talkative; I suppose she must have been a couple of years older than I. She helped me to settle down during my brief stay with them and was delegated to be my guide on the next stage of my escape.

Less than 24 hours after arriving it was time for me to move on, for what should be merely a walk across the border. At 3.30am I awoke from a deep sleep and quickly dressed. I then went into the kitchen where I found a young Russian soldier standing quietly to one side of the room. He spoke a little German and we were able to converse about my journeyings thus far. The daughter soon joined us however, and explained our intended plan of action over the next few hours. She introduced me to Vladimar, the Russian soldier, her boyfriend, who would be conducting us past all the sentries. Once clear of them however, we would be on our own.

"Ah Anni, good morning, I hope you've had a good night. Today we have a plan, but first we must give you a proper breakfast, before you set off on your journey with Susie and Vladimar."

We all sat at a big wooden table with a beautiful tablecloth. Coffee was served, or milk if we preferred, followed by a porridge, and after that a boiled egg with some nice brown bread.

Sandwiches were prepared for our journey and a bottle of beer was provided for our liquid sustenance. It was still dark when we three slipped from the house.

We were immediately swallowed up in a fog equally as thick as the one when I had arrived. We could hardly see in front of our eyes but this time I was being guided by someone familiar with the territory over which we were passing. We walked through the little village in which my hosts lived without any problems and soon came upon a second village which I was informed was the last one before we came to a large field, on the other side of which lay the border. The Russian soldier would not accompany us through the latter village but he promised to meet us at the other end of the main street and then take us across the field.

As we two girls walked through the village on our own, we were chatting about all sorts of different things which our lives had thrown up. She was laughing at me, saying how innocent I was but then saying it was nice that such people still existed. I was very conscious however, that something was not quite right, and knew instinctively that there was something very much on her mind – and it wasn't my escape to the West. She kept saying that she would have to buy some cigarettes and matches, which seemed a daft statement when it was still dark and all the shops were closed. I did not understand what was afoot, but my senses went on further alert when, as we finally came to the last house in the street, she told me to wait right there at the gate, while she went to get these cigarettes. It was only 5.30 in the morning and yet she walked up to the door and rang the bell. I couldn't believe it. I asked myself why she should be doing this at a time like this. It didn't make sense. Why couldn't I have gone along with her? I was scared, left out there in the street alone and my heart started to race as I weighed up the situation. She assured me that she would not be long and said that if anything untoward happened while I was awaiting her return I was to call for her. She then disappeared through the darkened doorway.

I walked up and down. I looked here and there, but there was no one in sight even though it was starting to grow lighter. The chances of discovery seemed to be increasing with every passing minute. I was prepared to wait – but then I had no obvious alternative. Minutes went by and after half-an-hour I was still waiting. Had I been abandoned? Should I shout for my guide or would she pretend not to hear me? My concern increased as the waiting went on.

Suddenly I was awoken from my thoughts and my increasing panic by the sound of a voice addressing me and the pressure of a rifle poking into my chest. I could hardly make out the man's silhouette in the thick fog swirling about us, and I'd certainly not heard him approaching. It was a Russian soldier yes; but not our friend Vladimar. His voice was harsh and sharp, and his countenance filled me with an instant foreboding. He spoke firstly in Russian but when he realised I did not understand what he was saying he switched to a broken form of German. He wanted to know what I was doing so near to the sentries and the border at this time of day. I recalled having once been told that if I should ever be in this sort of situation I should say that I was going over to the West to fetch leather jackets for the Russians. It was difficult to explain this to him, but I also raised my voice to a very loud shout in the hope that my guide would hear and come out to assist me.

The sound of the window behind me suddenly being thrown open interrupted our conversation and through the fog we could just make out the faces of my guide and a young Russian officer peering out. The officer, who could be identified as such by a peaked cap sitting jauntily atop a pile of fair curls, told the sentry to depart and leave me alone. Once the soldier had done so, my female guide addressed me. "Don't worry Anni, I'll soon be out. Sorry to have been such a long time." There were stifled giggles from the pair of them and the window was pulled to as they disappeared from my sight. I was very relieved at the sudden release of tension, but at the same time angry that I'd been forced to wait so long.

My guide made all sorts of excuses when she rejoined me, but it didn't take much imagination to realise what she and the Russian officer had been up to. It was not long before we were also joined by Vladimar although the near perfect timing of his return set me thinking.

We talked about the war together and he expressed the fond wish, which he felt was shared by the majority of Russian people, that the war should be confined to the past and that we should all live happily together. We walked along the streets past the sentries, not rushing or appearing agitated but behaving like we were courting – a soldier out late with a couple of girls. After about an hour's walk, we passed the last sentry position and he bade us farewell. He hugged us both and wished us luck for the future. I thought he was an honest upright citizen and he made me realise that there was good in every community. He had certainly changed my concept of the Russian soldier because none of my previous encounters with them had filled me with feelings other than of contempt. He waved and we waved back. He then strolled back up the street making his way back to his quarters, and we were alone.

The fog had not lifted but it was by now much lighter, and it was therefore a little easier to see where we were going. We had left the road however, and we had to be very careful where we were treading. My luggage was becoming heavier with every step, and as we slipped and slithered across the wet grass, feet twisting and plunging into crevices between the tufts, our position seemed to be becoming more and more desperate. Now and again we stopped, sat down to rest, talked and ate the few nibbles we had brought with us. Our clothing was wet and our hair bedraggled, and there was no sign that our journey was any nearer its end. For all I knew we could have been going in circles because I could see no obvious landmarks with the lifting fog still limiting visibility over any significant distance. We were both hungry, tired and cold.

It was hard going for me, because I was wearing several clothes and carrying a case as well.

"How much further, Susie? It seems such a long way. Are you sure this is the right way?"

Now she took a turning but she did not know if it was the right one, because we could not see due to the thick fog!

"I think we have to turn further to the left; I remember that's where the village is."

"Oh, so you've been here before! So you should know this area!" I said with disgust. But I was relying on her and dared not offend her.

"Of course, Anni, last year I took a few people across."

All at once, when my spirits were fairly deflated and I was lost in my own thoughts, my companion suddenly shouted, "We're here. I can see the village. Let's run." The idea that our journey was just about over gave us renewed energy and in spite of my encumbrances we started to run hell-for-leather across the remaining stretch of meadowland. Suddenly there was shooting all about us, and we flung ourselves headlong into the grasses. We lay flat and quiet. We didn't know where the shooting had come from, but we assumed it was from the German-Russian police. There was no follow up burst of fire and no one came to look. Face down, we lay there many awhile speaking in whispers, wondering what was going on and what to do next. The silence was eerie and yet we couldn't fathom out what might be happening. We couldn't lie in the field forever though. When everything was quiet and we deemed it safe to do so, we suddenly leapt up together and raced into the village.

Our arrival in the village went without further incident and once we had the comfort of the houses around us we stopped running. This was home territory for my guide and she knew these people as relatives, friends and neighbours. She was hailed warmly by a couple as we strolled along but generally we shunned anywhere that might mean us meeting people. Eventually, when I felt I could carry my case no further, she shepherded me into a farmhouse where I was introduced to all the occupants. New plans were immediately placed on my agenda, and again I had to wait around until the time was right for them to be put into effect. The farmer's wife came into the kitchen and gave us both something to eat. She explained that it was carnival time and everybody was busy cooking and baking for the event. It was also dangerous for me to be there, and I was transferred into the baking room. This was a hive of activity with everybody rolling out bread and rolls or making delicious-looking cakes. It was interesting to watch, but I had to be careful to keep away from the window so that I could not be seen by anybody who might be outside.

I stayed in there all afternoon. I was tired and there was nowhere there that I could rest. I had only one wish during my brief stay and that was to get moving and away from the place. This was not a reflection on their hospitality but just a deep desire to get away from the border region where my freedom could yet be snatched from me. At 5 o'clock that afternoon it was time for me to depart. Everything had been arranged, and a sweet gentleman from the farm was deputed to take me to the railway station at Giessen. And so we went off in an old car, speeding along fields, farms and beautiful countryside. It was autumn and the trees looked colourful with leaves of gold and orange. He liked me and didn't want me to go, but I told him that I had to as I was expected in Hilden. I thanked him again and told him also to thank Susie for her assistance. We said our farewells and he wished me luck before he melted into the crowds outside the station forecourt.

I strolled confidently through the station entrance and bought a single ticket to Hilden in the Rhineland. When I arrived in Giessen the carnival procession was right outside the station and there were hundreds of people everywhere. They were wearing masks, laughing joyously, and were dressed up in fancy costumes. I had paid them little attention when I arrived because I'd been more concerned about purchasing my ticket and catching the first train out. However, as I moved away from the ticket office, German-Russian police appeared as if from nowhere and surrounded everybody in sight. There were lots of people pushing and shoving and in the general turmoil I fled into an outside toilet. It was one of the old fashioned ones which did not flush and it reeked appallingly. It was absolutely filthy but I had no alternative than to stay put. I was able to see a fair bit of what was going on through a small hole in the wooden door. What I saw did not fill me with any real confidence. People were scurrying everywhere, and the police were stopping everyone they saw and examining their papers. Any without papers were being marched away.

I suppose I must have been in the toilet for over an hour before things started to quieten down. Luckily nobody had wanted to use the facility while I was in there, and nobody had thought to come in and search. After the general hubbub had died down and with darkness beginning to fall, I decided it was probably safe for me to emerge from my hiding place, and I made my way into the waiting room which was crowded with prospective travellers. Some of them were asleep while others were chatting away excitedly. There was little room but I walked up to a table where a young woman with a small boy was sitting. I gave them a smile of greeting and put down my case beside the only vacant chair. I then went over to purchase a drink from the counter and returned to sit down opposite them. The lady and I started chatting together and I warmed to her fairly quickly. I confided in her that I had no identity papers and that I was frightened in case a patrol passed by or that there might be some sort of check on our papers before the train could be boarded.

My drink was almost finished when my worst fears were realised. The first hint of trouble was the sound of marching boots and of raised voices, loud harsh voices of some officious authority which were coming our way. They were challenging people and had reached the glazed main doorway of the waiting room before I could move. I could see that they were German-Russian police and that they had my only escape route, the door, covered. All the tables in the waiting room were laid with long white tablecloths and my confidant suddenly said, "Quickly! Get under the table and hide until your train comes." I slid easily off my seat and hastily crouched down under the table hoping that anybody who had seen my sudden disappearance would not betray me. I heard some recalcitrant voices raised over to one side of the room and then their owners being made to leave in police custody. When they came over to our table I could only see, under the edge of the tablecloth, the shining boots of one of the men speaking to the lady with whom I had earlier been conversing. I was trembling with fear. I could see my reflection in the shine so close was he standing. Hardly had they arrived and looked fleetingly at my companion's papers than there was a commotion over in one corner, and they hurried over to help their colleagues who were struggling to restrain a group of people shouting and screaming at the injustice of their detention. It seemed others were objecting violently to their arrest and were being removed from the waiting room very much against their will. The distraction however meant that no further checking was conducted and there was some relief as the vociferous objectors were shepherded into the distance.

Everything then went quiet and even the people in the waiting room didn't start talking straight away stung into silence presumably by the trauma which had unfurled before them. However, the young lady eventually whispered to me that it was safe to come out, that it was all over, and that I should be making haste because the train for Hilden was just arriving in the station. I crawled out from under the table and picked up my luggage. I thanked the lady profusely for her assistance, and hurried out to board the train.

The compartment was full of young and old men. They were drinking and laughing and singing. They seemed very happy. They offered me a drink which at first I refused, but because they seemed such decent folk and I was feeling so happy to be at last on this train to freedom and a new life, I finally accepted their profferings. Anyway, I did not wish to appear churlish or a spoilsport just in case I needed their help later on during the journey, so I drank from the same bottle and joined in their songs. As it transpired, they all got off before I did, and waved, laughing and friendly, as they left the carriage. They were replaced by people who kept themselves to themselves and no further conversation was struck up. We could not have looked a very elegant bunch slumped as we were about the carriage as if in a drugged stupor, each of us lost in our own thoughts. I just stared blindly out of the window repelled somewhat by the sweaty odour of the large man squeezed up against me.

The train stopped at various places, grating to a climactic halt where it reposed in brooding silence seemingly determined never to move again; but each time it would gird up its loins and set off laboriously with much screeching of wheels, hissing of steam and billowing clouds of smoke which filled the nostrils. I took my sandwiches from my bag and ate heartily. After approximately two hours travel, when we were not far from Vohwinkel, a tall well-made German-Russian policeman appeared at the entrance to the compartment and announced loud and importantly, "Identity cards please. Come on now, as quickly as possible." I had not expected this at all. Next to me was this huge fat man who had his back turned towards me and who I had earlier been silently cursing for his odour. Now I welcomed his bulk as I tried to burrow beneath his huge frame, sinking myself into the narrow niche created between the seat, his back and the carriage wall. I gazed fearfully out towards the window through the small gap which remained and waited. My heart was pounding away. The policeman walked along the aisle, nodded to everyone, and generally seemed quite satisfied. The gentleman next to me showed him his papers and then cracked some jokes with him distracting his attention. It seemed to work because the policeman then moved on to the next compartment.

After he had gone, the fat gentleman turned to me and looked at me questioningly. I could not avoid his look as he slid his bulk sideways all the better to see me. His face broke into a broad smile and he said, "I presume that you have no Identity card Fraulein." "No, I'm afraid not," I stuttered, and then tried to explain. "No my dear. There is no need for explanations. I could tell that you were very frightened when I got on the train, but have no fear now. I will do my best to protect you for the rest of the journey." It was really nice of him and I thanked him profusely.

Yet again I had been very lucky in my travelling companions. It must be said that in all of my journeyings I met a lot of really nice people who were willing to help me, to give me sustenance and generally to ease me on my way. My new found fat friend, however, warned me that there was invariably trouble at the barrier in Hilden, in the western part of the Rhineland. He advised me to alight as soon as the train stopped and to run as fast as I could through the ticket barrier where there would be further checks of identity cards.

At Hilden I did just that. I climbed down from the train, hiding anonymously amongst the crowd that had alighted with me. I could see a lot of people at the barrier, where arguing and shouting had broken out. The controller had his back to me and was remonstrating with a lady. This seemed the best opportunity I was likely to get so, remembering what my fat man had told me I took to my heels – through the barrier, out of the station, and into the West. I'd made it at last!

Chapter 12
My First Taste of Freedom

I had been given the address of a family in Hilden, called Breuer, who I was to seek out on my arrival at the Bahnhof – main station. From there it was necessary for me to catch a tram and as it was 6 o'clock in the morning, everybody was setting out on their way to work. The tram was absolutely packed with people although, as I looked out at all the bombed and desolate buildings, I couldn't imagine where they could all be heading. Still! That was not my problem. I'd reached my stop. I alighted from the tram in accord with the detailed instructions that I'd been given and had a short distance to walk. I had no trouble in finding their house. In fact, Frau Breuer was already outside in her garden. She was a plump friendly person to whom I quickly warmed. She introduced me to her husband who welcomed me into the house. They continued chatting and listening to my ramblings, while Frau Breuer prepared and brought me a bowl of soup and some bread. I can only remember eating two spoonfuls of the soup before collapsing where I sat. I was absolutely exhausted and I slept for hours and hours.

When I finally awoke after that much needed sleep, Frau Breuer brought me some breakfast and opened the curtains of the bedroom to which they had carried me the previous evening. The sun came flooding in. It was a miracle that I was here, but now I was and the sun seemed to be heralding a new dawning. I figured that the worst was now behind me, but little did I know that there were still difficulties to be overcome.

Frau Breuer and I talked about my starting work and it was suggested that she take me to a friend of hers who owned a jewellery shop. She knew that they were seeking somebody to cook for both the family and their staff and with my parents having been in the same trade she had some idea that I might be well suited – the relevance between my cooking capabilities and my parents' jewellery shop was not apparent to me. Still! Work was work. The cleaning was already being performed by an elderly gentleman but he was so busy that he could not take on any other duties. I agreed to become this family's chief cook and bottle – washer because, without any papers, there was no way I could obtain a job through normal channels. In those days the Government of West Germany would not permit people to cross over from the East, the law which was to permit this only being introduced quite some time later. Because I came from the East, there was no way I could obtain the relevant documentation and I was thus in the West as an illegal immigrant unable to adopt a normal lifestyle.

Accordingly, the following day I made my way to Frau Lindemann who took me into her employ. In accord with the West German laws of the time, any refugee who entered the West Zone would be deported immediately upon discovery to the East Zone whence they came. This was considered to be sufficient and suitable punishment for potential lawbreakers and adequate discouragement to those who might be tempted. It was out of the question therefore for any refugee to seek to obtain work legally. The only hope for them was to know somebody who would put them in touch with an employer willing to engage a refugee. The trouble with such a policy was that this led to the widespread and dreadful exploitation of anyone in the sector illegally. However, there was nothing they could do about it. If they complained they would be dispatched back to the East where they knew far worse living conditions existed.

The Breuer's had arranged for me to work in the Lindemann's kitchen as a cook, and for that I will always be grateful. It was hard work however, very poorly paid, and the lady of the house was a very nasty person – an objectionable piece of work. I had to put up with her incessant rantings and ravings though, because there was nowhere else for me to go and, anyway, I'd been through far worse. Weeks went by and my disillusionment with the job grew and grew. I was up at 6.30am so that breakfast was ready for the family at 7 o'clock and I would not be finished until 9 or 10 o'clock in the evening. I was allowed only one afternoon off per week but even then I had to return in time to prepare the family's evening meal. When Frau Lindemann's mother was taken sick and she had to visit her for a few days I took the opportunity to venture out in search of other employment. On the evening of her return to the family house, I informed Frau Lindemann that I would be leaving. She was furious with me, but I pointed out the severity of the conditions under which she had made me work and how I found them intolerable. I was being treated no better than a slave.

I left her employ and went to work for an English family. I was not familiar with their type of food however, and had great difficulty in cooking it successfully and to their satisfaction. I was asked to leave there as a consequence, but found further employment with another

English family. It turned out to be a case of "out of the frying pan into the fire", because there I was treated no better than a common criminal. The family had an Alsatian bitch and a litter of her puppies. Regularly a large saucepan of porridge had to be prepared for the animals and to me it looked positively revolting. Having cooked it I then had to serve it up for the dogs but I was never allowed any breakfast for myself. In the early days I asked humbly if I could have something to eat, but the response I received from my employer was that if I wanted anything then I would have to share the dogs' porridge. Since I was starving I had no alternative but to eat it. A similar scenario would be enacted every dinner time too. The tasty aroma of good wholesome food would fill the kitchen setting my salivary glands going in anticipation, but the dishes of food would then be transported into the living room. Everybody, including the German nanny, would file into the living room to eat, but if I attempted to follow suite, the lady of the house would scream at me and banish me to the kitchen. I would then sit in the kitchen listening to their convivial banter feeling rejected and starving.

The only food my mistress would allow me was what was left on the family's plates after they had had their fill. Since I couldn't live without food and could not complain to anyone, I had to obey their demands and filch whatever scraps I could to survive. I was up at 6 o'clock every morning to get breakfast. I would then scrub the carpets, wash all the floors, and help in the bedrooms making the beds and tidying round. They had two small children, the youngest of which was only one year old. The husband was an officer and very pleasant person when he was on his own. I was expected to clean all the buttons on his uniform and make sure his shoes shone daily. His wife on the other hand, was a completely different kettle of fish. She was a small, dark person, forever smoking and drinking, who seemed to become hysterical over the littlest bit of a thing. She shouted, she screamed, and would make me clean something twice or three times if the mood so took her.

One Friday, she decided that all the furniture in her bedroom should be moved so that I could clean behind the wardrobes. None of the family were around, however, and the nurse gave me a helping hand. When we tried to move one of the wardrobes it started to tip over slightly but I was able to catch it in time. The lady of the house chose that very moment to enter the room and was just in time to see the one-year old baby crawling across the floor and into the line where the wardrobe appeared to be tipping. She ran across from the doorway, grabbed the tot up from the floor, and accused me of trying to murder her baby. I was shocked at her suggestion that I was deliberately trying to harm her family but she was not willing to listen to any sort of explanation. The nurse didn't stick up for me, and I was ordered from the house. I was fired, and she wanted me out of the house within the next few minutes. I was stunned and ran crying to my room to gather up my things. I packed my case and then went to see her to ask for the money in payment for all the hard work I had already put in that week. She just laughed and spat in my face. She refused to pay me anything. I suppose I should have been forewarned.

When I'd first taken up the appointment, I had been shown to my room on that first day, and found stuffed under the mattress on my bed, broken up bread, some of it fresh, some stale and some downright mouldy. It should have triggered my normally acute sense of impeding trouble, but I suppose that I'd been so relieved at obtaining a position I'd put aside any misgivings. I had ignored the obvious sufferings of the previous incumbent because I could not have believed that an English person would treat someone other than in an understanding and compassionate manner. How disappointed I was that my illusions had been so cruelly shattered. The fact that she refused to pay me was the final straw.

I walked out of the house with my little suitcase in one hand and a smaller bag in the other. I crossed the road, turned the corner so that I was out of sight of the obnoxious woman if she happened to be looking and collapsed onto my suitcase with my hands covering my face to conceal the tears which were by then streaming uncontrollably. Fate seemed to keep inflicting heavy blows upon my tiring frame and I was wondering how many more I could take. When I eventually looked up I discovered that a crowd of people had gathered around me. They were concerned about my welfare and queried what I was doing here on the street alone. I felt utterly despondent. I had nowhere to go, no money, no food and no home. I seemed to have reached an all-time low. The German social job centre who had helped me obtain the position from which I had just been fired, were unlikely to be able to help me again, and I did not anticipate I would get much of a reference from the family I'd just left. What was I to do?

Suddenly I became aware of a young man pushing his way through the crowd and shouting: "Anni, whatever are you doing here?

You must come with me and I will take you back to my parents' home." I could hardly believe my good fortune. It was the son of the Breuer's. I was so happy to see him that I got up and ran to him, grabbing him in a warm embrace. My face lit up with delight. He was my knight in shining armour at that particular moment, and together we strolled through the streets to his parent's house. Frau and Herr Breuer were very surprised to see me and strongly advised me that, in the future, I should look for a job only with German people because, although it was by now some three years since the end of the War, the English still felt a lot of hatred towards the German population. Furthermore, it was about this time that the law was also changed and it became possible for refugees to work legally in the West Zone.

The following morning I travelled to Cologne in search of work. I went to the so-called job centre and was sent to a small farm-house miles away from the city centre. They were very nice people but they had eight children and I realized that I just would not be able to cope with such a large family. They were very good to me and fed me, and then kindly showed me the way back to Cologne.

It was late afternoon when I arrived back in the city centre and I visited a few shops enquiring after work, all to no avail. I wandered through the streets hardly cognizant of my surroundings until I became aware of little faces eyeing me from a nearby cellar. The buildings all around me were totally bombed to the ground and there were nothing but ruins. I had not considered that people might have to live in such squalor but, for a large number of people, the cellars of bombed buildings offered the only shelter. This was where thousands lived, slept, cooked and survived for a very long time. Even then, three years after the War, people were being forced to live amongst the dereliction and devastation with little immediate hope of a brighter future. Until that moment I had not given the matter much thought, being more concerned with my own predicament, but those faces peering up from their hole in the ground made a lasting impression on my consciousness. The place was eerie and I was scared. I looked up at the sky and could see but one building silhouetted against the skyline in the slowly darkening glow provided by the setting sun. It was the Cologne cathedral. Apart from some damage to, I believe, the west wing it was largely intact. It was good to see the cathedral because it was both a calming influence and a visible symbol for me that God was not far from my side.

It was getting late and I had no idea where I might be able to rest for the night. I was also becoming very tired from all my exertions since arriving in Cologne. I found myself near to the main hospital in Cologne and I thought that I could perhaps have one last try there for a job. As I walked up the path towards the main gate two nuns were approaching me from the opposite direction. They were talking and laughing, and sounded so happy. I stopped them with the intention of asking if they knew whether any help was needed at the hospital, but I suddenly choked up and collapsed at their feet. My hunger and tiredness had finally caught up with me.

The nuns gathered me up and took me straight inside. They gave me food and a bed for the night, and the following morning I was invited into the office of the Mother Superior. She offered me a job on their switchboard, which also involved acting as receptionist for patients attending the hospital as outpatients, and with appointments to see the doctor. I loved the job and made friends with the girls with whom I shared the bedroom.

The hospital was called the St Vincent Hospital, and attached to it was a nunnery. The chapel had been donated by the holy St Vincent, and everyone had to gather there for prayers at six o'clock every morning. A short mass was said, after which we were all allowed to have breakfast which consisted generally of porridge and a cup of milk. It never seemed to be enough for me – the prayers lasted longer than the breakfasts. I did not understand much about the Catholic faith at that time but I have always believed in God. I took up lessons in the Catholic faith but I did not finish them at that time. I was determined to become a Catholic later in my life but I've learned from experience that nothing comes easily in this life. I had to fight hard for it but it was some eight years after the War ended before my wish was finally fulfilled and I was accepted into that religion.

I liked the job at the hospital but I knew it could never be permanent. It belonged to a lady who was absent through illness and after several weeks in the post, I had to relinquish it. The Mother Superior could offer me no other work and I had no option than to go back out into the big wide world.

It was becoming a lonely, hostile place and in the little free time I'd had I had not been able to trace my parents during my sojourn in the West. I was thus forced to seek further employment wherever it could be found and trust that God would lead me out of the wilderness. I was offered a job as a domestic help by a family living in

Benrath near Dusseldorf. The mother was called Helga, the father Rolf. I quite enjoyed my period with them. I was not expected to be a skivvy for a pittance and I was getting reasonable time to myself. Indeed, conditions generally in West Germany were improving and normality was starting to gain the upper hand.

A young woman, Emma, was employed part-time to do the cleaning, washing and ironing, while I helped prepare food for the meals and Helga would go out shopping. Emma and I got on together really well. She lived only a few houses away, with her mother and little girl, and on my day off she would invite me there. I enjoyed my life with Helga and Rolf. Often we got together in the evenings and we would play games or talk about the war. However, I didn't tell them that I was Jewish, because I didn't know how they would feel about it. They were Catholics and Helga allowed me to go with her to church on Sunday mornings.

Christmas was slowly approaching and everything was decorated in festive spirit. After Helga had done her shopping she came into the kitchen with a big Christmas cake—a *stollen*. I felt a little lonely without my father and mother and my only sister and I thought back to how we always celebrated Christmas.

Finally Christmas arrived and there was a lot to do, preparing the meal, cleaning and washing up. On Christmas Eve afternoon Helga and Rolf asked me to come to their room and they gave me a lovely present: a necklace with a small cross in silver which I didn't expect, and some chocolate and a little marzipan pig. Later we sang Christmas songs and played games. We were all very happy, laughing and talking. On Christmas Eve evening we heard the bells ringing from a nearby church, and eventually we all turned in.

After Christmas I worked a few more weeks. It was in the middle of the day whilst I was busy cleaning that the doorbell rang and I went to answer it. I opened the door – and there stood my sister Jutta. I couldn't believe it at first. I was amazed and astounded. She had tracked me down and was able to give me news of our parents, with whom she was living. They had moved to Hanover where they had managed to build up a new and profitable business, and they would love to have me return home. I was on a high! The two of us spent the whole day together, initially finishing off my chores and then making plans for my reunion with the family.

I had to give a week's notice to my employer. The day finally arrived when I had to leave these lovely people. Even the dogs looked sad. Somehow, with a heavy heart, I walked slowly downstairs, opened the big door and started my journey back to the Breuers in Hilden, where I had left a few things behind, and stayed with them for a further week.

On the Saturday the Breuers, the parents and the son, accompanied me to the station and we promised to keep in touch with each other. They both stood on the platform shedding tears as the train started to pull out of the station.

"Goodbye, Anni, take care" were the last words I could make out before they were drowned out by the huffing and puffing of the train as it hauled itself noisily out of the station and they slowly faded into the distance. I waved for a very long time until they became so small in the distance that I could no longer discern them. Parting at railway stations was not new to me and seems to have punctuated my life with a monotonous regularity, but it became no easier with each subsequent one. This departure signalled yet another chapter of my life which was closing and I knew that the next was only just around the corner. After all the setbacks of previous "new" beginnings I was more confident than ever that this really would be the rebirth of the life so harshly denied me since those early innocent days in Kołobrzeg and Krakov.

I could hardly contain myself at thoughts of the imminent reunion with my parents, and the journey took all too long. Would they be proud of me? I would have many stories to recount to them, and I hoped that they would not be disappointed in me.

My mother was already on the platform waiting for me when the train pulled into Hanover. She was a smart as ever, and her smile and bright eyes reflected her pleasure at my homecoming. We embraced and then she took me home. It was truly fabulous to be a whole family once again, reunited under the same roof. Nevertheless, the euphoria could not last forever and plans still had to be made for our future. Hanover had not been reconstructed and unemployment was high. No one could not but worry about the future, but as a united family once again I certainly felt that we would be able to conquer all the might beset us. After 10 years of torment and separation we were at last back together with hope in our hearts and love and happiness in our souls.

First I had to get a job so that I could support my parents. Jutta was already working for the chambers of commerce; she was very clever. She arranged for me to take a typing and shorthand course, which lasted for six months. After that I was ready to apply for work in an office.

I was lucky, and on the 30th May I was offered a job to work for the British in an office called DPACCS, a displaced persons camp (in post-World War II). The office supported refugees from Eastern Europe and the former prisoners of the Nazi concentration camps. They had a choice to go to France, Belgium or Greece. Those who were willing and easily repatriated were quickly returned to their country of origin. After a year the DPACCS had to close down since it was only authorized for a limited time. I enjoyed my job and met so many refugees who were in such a sorry state but happy to be found a new home.

I also met my future husband, Philip Dean, there. He was in the British Army at the time and frequently came to deliver post or documents. As he was coming in or leaving he always gave me a nice smile, which I returned. Then one time just before the end of the day, he asked me if he could take me out sometime. I agreed, and we started courting. My father was not very pleased since he thought the soldier was too young for me. But I carried on going out with him despite that.

My first husband

In 1949, I found another job with a German company who needed a shorthand typist with some knowledge of the English language. I worked with other clerks and soon made friends. During the wintertime a caretaker would come and light a fire in a large old-fashioned stove, since the office was so big and cold. I worked there for two years and was very sorry to leave. Philip wanted to make arrangements for our engagement and planned for me to travel to

England where we would get married, and on 13th May 1951 we got engaged.

We would go for long walks and had meals in some nice forest restaurants. Then out of the blue my parents told me to stop seeing him. My father said: "Why do you need to make up your mind so quickly? You are young and can wait till you meet somebody else." We argued every day; I told him that I loved Philip. But after more shouting and arguing I got up from supper, went into my bedroom and slammed the door. My father said: "If you won't give up this stupid affair, you had better leave the house."

I had a very good friend who helped me to collect my belongings and took me to her home. It was a very small place—she lived there with her mother because her dad had been killed in the war. I knew that I couldn't stay there for very long, and so started looking for a

In Hanover, 1953

place of my own. I saw an advert for a Caritas[2] home where there was a place available. I went there straight away and a very nice lady

---

2 A Catholic social charity

interviewed me. Sharing a room with the other girls was no problem for me. We got on very well and often talked late into the night.

At that time I wasn't sure if I would be able to get married, but my fiancée took me to Hamburg to apply for a UK visa, though I had to wait for three months in case I changed my mind. Philip returned to England during this time.

The decision was made and the big day came on 31st July 1951 when my parents and my sister took me to the train station. We hugged each other and, with tears in my eyes, I stepped onto the train and waved until my family grew smaller and further away. After this journey I would never see my parents again.

I travelled to Hamburg to start my journey into a future unknown. When I arrived in Hamburg I collected my ticket to board the ship at 7.30p.m. and I was shown to my cabin. The ship was an English freight ship called the Empire Baltic. This was the only ship that my fiancée could arrange as nothing else was available at the time. There were only a few other ladies on board who were all travelling for different reasons, and at night we were invited for a drink. The crew was very friendly with us, but it was soon time to retire to bed. In the morning I was offered a cup of tea and I thought how nice this was.

Chapter 13
A New Life in Sheffield, England

I saw the first lights which were getting more visible the nearer we got to England. It seemed so welcoming to me and I was happy to have arrived safely. Lots of seagulls surrounded the ship making their usual chatter. I had breakfast with the other ladies and the ship's captain.

We were all talking and laughing when, all of a sudden, my fiancée appeared at Tilbury Docks. We embraced and I said my last goodbyes to everyone on the ship. We both walked to the station and in Tilbury caught the final train to Sheffield, where he took me to his home.

I was introduced to Philip's parents who made me comfortable, and I stayed at their house before our wedding. Phillip's parents owned a newsagent's shop at 51 Infirmary Road, which we eventually took over. I was somehow disappointed with the area, because I had lived in better areas in Germany. But I thought, at least I am in England and I will get used to the lifestyle eventually.

The shop on Infirmary Road

We got married on 13th August 1951; I became Mrs Dean and was very proud to be his wife. After the wedding and the everyday chores, I was shown how to manage the shop, marking up the papers which the paper boys would deliver. I found that I could not decipher the money, since I was used to decimals, but soon I got used to it.

The first four years we had no children. I was really upset about this, but one day I felt unwell, then my stomach was upset for 3 months. I went to see a doctor who confirmed that I was pregnant. When I got home I told my husband the great news. "Philip, I am pregnant at last."

He said, "What? Just when we are getting busy in the shop. What are we going to do?"

This upset me badly, I thought he would be pleased. My mother-in-law never offered to help. When I was six months on, I still had to get up at 5 in the morning to mark up the papers, while my dear husband carried on sleeping. I went upstairs and took all the bedding down and told him to get up. He just went back to bed with all the bedding. I told my in-laws about it and they told him off for not helping. But he was not bothered, and in the mornings the workers helped me to carry in the load of papers.

Serving in the shop

When I started having labour pains and became restless, he shouted at me, saying: "for goodness sake, I can't sleep with you moaning." I went downstairs, but the pain got worse. I shouted "come down, I think the baby is on its way." He came down and ordered an ambulance. Soon I was taken to the hospital, but he didn't come with me. My baby was born at 3 o'clock, with fair hair and blue eyes. This was our Margaret, a lovely little girl.

Philip seemed happy and managed the shop, but when our daughter was one year old he decided to sign on for the army. This meant that I had to look after a small child and a shop as well. I told him this was not fair, but he didn't listen.

When he came home everything seemed to be all right. After two years I was pregnant again, and in 1958 our son David was born. We were happy and this time Philip was more helpful. When he came out of the army he got a job in a hardware shop. I worked in the newsagent's shop as much as I could, because we had to earn money.

When Philip came home from work he said, "I want a footbath, my feet are killing me. Can't you do this?"

"No."

"But all English women do that here." And I believed him. "Now dry them, hurry up. Have you got my tea ready?"

I said I was busy and he smacked me then.

"I'm hungry, get me something to eat." This happened every night. If we were having our dinner and someone came into the shop he would say "Shop!" and I would go to serve again. If several customers came in, I told him to help and he would say, "Can't you see I'm reading the paper?"

This went on for weeks and months. Another time he wanted to know where his socks were, and as I turned round to give them to him, he smacked me hard in the face. It got worse. One night our baby cried and cried, and eventually I got up to fetch him from his cot, but Philip was there first and threw me onto the bed and tried to strangle me. I struggled, but he was stronger. I thought I was going to die. The baby kept crying and gradually I pushed him back. He realised he had gone too far.

Our newsagent's shop was full of customers, but I couldn't serve them any more, as I was on the verge of a breakdown. A good friend, Paula, came to help me, serving people in the shop. She asked: "Where is he?"

"He's gone to his mother."

"You shouldn't put up with this, love. You can come to me until we have sorted something out."

The following morning, after Philip had left for work, I grabbed a few things, and clothes for the babies. I was told later that he was shocked and wanted to know where I had gone.

After leaving Philip I went to stay with Paula, who lived alone, and we got on really well. Since she was not working, she looked after my children while I searched for a job to help with our upkeep and bills. I found work in an office, which I had to do full time, otherwise I would not have made enough money to pay my way. I was out all day, my children missed me and I missed them too, because they were very young.

I worked in that job for nearly a year, then decided that I would look for a housekeeping job where I could look after the children myself. Paula agreed with this plan and hoped that I would find something suitable. We both searched in the advertising columns for people who were looking for friendship and assistance. After a few days we found someone who wanted help with housekeeping, who seemed suitable. I went to this address straight after work. I knocked nervously on the door and a gentleman, who looked older than me, opened the door.  He was quite friendly and asked what I wanted. I told him that I had come for the housekeeping job and introduced myself. "Oh," he said, "come on in!" He had a dog that was well trained and stayed by his side.

"Tell me everything. Why would a young woman want to do this sort of work?" I told him then what had happened and he agreed for me to start whenever I was available. He was called Tom and he worked as a foreman in a factory. I told him that I had to give my notice first, but after a fortnight I was able to start this job as housekeeper and was able to live in, along with my children.

Tom was a widower and, with a big house, with the washing and the cooking, he could no longer manage. I went to see Paula; she was happy for me and we promised that we would see each other again as soon as I had settled in. My children were so happy to have their mum look after them again. Tom was happy too because when he came from work the meal was always on the table, and he liked my cooking and baking, and the house was transformed into a nice clean place.

When Tom was on afternoon shifts I had more time to spend with the children. I took Margaret, the eldest, to school for her first day. I was so glad that I could take her myself rather than leaving it to Paula, even though she was very good with the children. Tom liked the children too and spoiled them somewhat.

After a few months I got my divorce through and I was free again. Philip married again but he and his new wife didn't seem happy. Later he suffered a heart attack and died in hospital, at the age of only forty-nine.

For a time Tom and I lived happily together with the children, then one evening he proposed to me. With a trembling voice he said, "Anni, will you marry me?" I was surprised but I thought that finally there would be security for me and the children, and after all we got on so well and would love each other over time. So I agreed, and we made plans for the wedding. It was only a small circle of friends, and of course Paula was invited too and she was happy for me.

We decided to leave that area and moved to a house with a nice garden where the children loved to play. Of course we had to change schools, but they made new friends. One year later our son Lawrence was born and this completed our family. Tom adored him, he was such a lovely baby and we all spoiled him. We really enjoyed our life, making trips to various places, though we couldn't really afford the luxury of travelling abroad.

Then one day Tom became ill. He seemed to have had lost weight, he had less appetite and felt so ill that he had to give up his job. He got worse with each day until the doctor confirmed he had cancer and had not long to live. After six months of suffering, Tom died. We were all devastated, but I had to stay strong to face whatever was ahead of me.

As time went by and the children got older, I was able to look for a job to enable me to pay the bills: for food, electric, gas, and of course the rent. In those days it was not too difficult to get a job. Since I had worked in an office before, I applied again for a job as an office clerk, and since my typing speed and also shorthand, which was in big demand at that time, were good, I was accepted, but only part-time. On Saturdays I was free, as were the children. I used to take them on various trips, or to a swimming bath or a zoo, which they really enjoyed. And since I was a good skater they got interested in skating, both outdoor and indoor.

One day I saw an advertisement in our local newspaper about an airshow in Finningley. I thought this would make a change, I told the children about it and asked if they would like to go. They were very excited and couldn't wait for the day to come. "OK," I said, "I will get some tickets," hoping they were not sold out.

When the Saturday approached we made our way to the coach stop and already many people, adults and children, were waiting. Everybody was talking and laughing and people were really friendly. We wondered what it was like out there on an airfield. The weather was nice but quite cool, with that nip in the air that made you realise that summer days were behind you and winter lay ahead. But the fresh cool wind didn't bother us.

It was all so busy we had to practically fight our way through the crowds. We also saw several stalls that offered cakes, ice cream, and other refreshments. I treated my children to whatever they wanted, and a souvenir of course.

I was looking round when I saw a huge plane and an airman talking to people. We waited until they had gone and slowly walking up to him. I asked politely if he could explain anything about the inside of this plane. My older son was very interested and started to ask questions.

"Of course", the airman said smiling, "it is my pleasure to help with whatever you want to know."

"What is a cockpit, sir", my son wanted to know.

"Right, son, I will explain how a cockpit works. It is a section of the plane where a pilot manages the aircraft with a panel of instruments and controls. These are used to take off, to land and to control the progress of the flight."

I moved slightly nearer to see and hear what the airman was explaining, when all of a sudden a plane flew over us with such a roar that in shock, I flew into his arms. "Oh, I'm so sorry," I apologized, "please forgive me." My children and the airman were all laughing at me and I felt embarrassed, but he was very understanding and told us a lot of people had the same experience.

"Tell me, didn't your husband want to come, or is he working perhaps?" he asked. "Forgive me for asking."

I explained to him that my husband had died a few years ago and that I now lived alone with my children. And then I asked, "What about you, then?" He told me he had lost his wife some years ago, too, and that his mother had to look after his children. "That is very noble of your mother to look after them," I said.

"Well, I had no other choice since I am in the Air Force, you know, and I have to travel."

"Well, children, we must go now or we will miss the coach," I said.

I thanked him for everything he had explained to us. The children were already waiting for me impatiently, and I told him that we must go as it was getting late. Many were already heading towards the coach and we made our way through the crowds. All at once somebody was shouting my name, and when I looked back I saw the airman again, who stopped me and wanted to know my address. "Please can I contact you?" I was surprised because I hardly knew him, but quickly gave him my address and he promised to get in touch.

We boarded the coach and made our way home. The children asked why he had stopped me and I said, "Because he wanted to see me again."

A few days later I received a letter from the airman. 'I like you and if you don't mind, would you write back to me. I am an aircraft mechanic and I also test planes to see if they are fit to fly. I live with my mother and my children, since my wife died some time ago. I have a car and could pick you up if this is all right with you? Sincerely, Ted.'

"Oh children, this airman wants to see me again. What do you say?"

"Write back, mother, he seems to be a decent chap."

I soon replied – that was by letter which was slow – I couldn't then afford such luxuries as a telephone, and mobiles had not yet been invented.

We started courting and got on well together. Then one day he asked me if I would marry him. I was reluctant to give him an answer straight away. After a few months he asked me again and told me how much he loved me, and this time I agreed.

A date was set and we told everybody we knew and sent out invitation cards. Ted's mother baked a fantastic wedding cake, decorated with a heart-shaped figure with two little birds. We got married in March 1974, surrounded by family and friends who wished us luck and a long life together with lots of happiness.

Ted and me

Soon after, we moved to a new house with a nice garden. The children liked Ted, so did our little cat who followed him around everywhere. We also had nice holidays and occasional days out.

One day a letter arrived. I was overjoyed to see that it was from Edith, my old school friend from Eisenach. She wanted to see me in Germany and she had also invited our school friend Lottie. I discussed it with Ted who was rather anxious about me making this journey, but he agreed and I wrote back to Edith to say that I would come. I booked a flight to Frankfurt and gave her the date and the time.

Finally, on a sunny day in June, I arrived in high spirits at the airport. I was not sure what to expect but I didn't have to worry, because as I came out I saw my two old friends Edith and Lottie waiting for me, eagerly waving. We embraced immediately and all started talking at the same time.

Then we took a train to Eisenach where Edith was still living. We walked out of the station and up a steep hill towards Edith's flat—there was no public transport to her area. We were exhausted by our long walk but finally got there and were welcomed to Edith's lovely flat, where she had already prepared a good and hearty meal for us.

"Come and make yourself at home. You must be hungry after such a long journey."

"Oh, thank you Edith, and this is delicious. But tell us, why are you no longer living in the hotel?"

Jutta, Edith and Anneliese

When we were all seated on her comfortable sofa. Edith told us her whole story.

"When the Russians occupied the town, they stormed into the hotel and demanded beer or any kind of alcohol, whatever was available. My father gave them what they wanted and as they left, quite tipsy, they shouted in an aggressive manner: "We'll be back soon!" They did come back the following day and wanted more beer, and wanted to know where I was: "Where is that little pretty one with black hair that we saw yesterday?" My father told them that his daughter had left, and he didn't know where she had gone. But they came back every day, wanting more beer until there was none left. Every day they got drunk and smashed furniture, laughing and shouting.

Later my father was advised to leave the hotel and was offered a job as a waiter at the Wartburg, a famous castle hovering over the town.

I could not return to the hotel because I was afraid of being raped, and stayed with a friend who lived not far away. But the Russians were doing a house-to-house in search of girls and women. The Russians came one evening and my friend's dad told them, "There are no girls here!" Now I had to find someone else who would hide me for a short time. I was lucky and found an elderly lady who knew my father, and often dined with him.

"Of course, dear," she said. "Come in and I will do my best to hide you when I think they are coming."

"Oh, thank you so much, I will repay your kindness if I can."

But suddenly one day, the elderly lady became ill and I had to find other accommodation, so I went to the housing department to make enquiries. After a lot of consideration, the housing official offered me a place, not far from Friedrichs Strasse, which was not a very nice area, but I accepted and went straight away. The place was dirty, and had no heating appliances, there was a window pane missing which caused a lot of draught. It was damp and unsafe. When the rain came it rained through the ceiling into my room and I couldn't sleep.

I decided then to go back to the housing people. I told them about the conditions, but all she could say was, "Put a bucket down then. We can't help because we have no workers to repair damaged properties. But come back tomorrow." I came back every day and every time the same answer was the same. I thought, I will try just once more, and sat down and waited. There were so many people that most of them had to stand for hours until they were attended to.

A young man who just walked in, asked me if he could sit next to me since he had an injured leg. We started a small conversation and I learned that he had been offered a flat and had come just to sign a few papers. "You are lucky then," I said, "because I am trying to get something decent, but they are not helping me."

This man was a little older than me and was very friendly. He said he could help me, but only for a limited time. "How can you help me?" I wanted to know. "You can have a room in my flat, if you want, we can share the rent. What do you say?" I was so desperate that I accepted straight away. "I am working but can you come tomorrow afternoon?" I agreed and thanked him profusely. The next day I left my flat and brought my few belongings. He was a real gentleman, helped me with my case and gave me some information about the house. At last I was safe and could sleep without getting cold.

After a few months we fell in love. We were courting for a while, then one day he asked me to marry him. I was so lucky, believe me. We were married with just a few friends at the wedding. We were happy, and were blessed with a son and a daughter, and life went on in a normal way.

But one day he didn't come home and I was worried when a policeman knocked on the door and gave me the grave news. He was involved in a car accident, taken to hospital, but it was too late. When he died I was devastated and shocked. All arrangements for his funeral were made and some of the mates he used to work with stood at my side. Some refreshments were laid and when I went home I thought how lucky I was to have my children to support me at that sad time."

"Thank you for your story, Edith, we are so sorry that you had to go through so much trauma," we said in unison.

Soon it was time to leave, our parting came too soon. As we said goodbye we thought about how much our lives had changed. It had been such a long journey for us all. The three of us were able to live, to survive and to thrive. Reflecting back, we must find patience in our lives, and trust God to lead us where we need to go.

Lottie's story, as retold by Anneliese

I am Lottie Schumann and my story begins in Berlin where I was born in 1929. My father was a lawyer and my mother worked in a textiles business. I had one older brother Rudi.

Our house was situated near a park, where we often went for walks. My maternal grandparents lived not far from our street, and so we were able to visit them often, or they would come to us. When the schools were closed for holidays, my grandmother used to take us on various trips.

We were a very happy family. But then war broke out and suddenly our lives were no longer happy and peaceful.

The Germans invaded Poland on 1st September 1939, and Britain and France declared war on Germany on 3rd September, because the Germans refused to stop the invasion. I was nearly ten when the bombing started in September 1939. The sirens howled across the city warning us to seek shelter in a cellar. This happened frequently.

In 1941 a law was passed requiring that every Jew who had reached the age of 6 must wear a star of yellow material inscribed with the word 'Jew'. This was a shock to my parents because my father was Jewish, but my mother was 'Aryan,' as the Nazis called non-Jews.

My father is taken away

My mother was in a daze, not able to decide if her husband should hide or not. But it was not long before the Gestapo arrived at our house; I think in late 1941. The men were ruthless and started kicking my father. I screamed and shouted to let him go, to stop it, but there was nothing I could do. My mother slammed the front door and ran after him to give him the warm coat which he might need, but the men refused and my dear papa left without his coat.

After they had gone I had to calm my mother down, I tried to console her. "Lottie," she said, "I am going to see grandma and grandpa and ask what our next step should be, because I am afraid that the Gestapo might want to speak to me as well."

Grandma was very upset, but she said she would have a word with a friend of my father, and next day she went to see him.

This friend was very sympathetic and promised to help us. Grandma said, "but how, what can you do?"

"Leave it with me, love," he said, "and I will let you know as soon as possible."

"Oh thank you, Herr Schwind"

"Call me Otto, Frau Schumann, and I'll see you soon."

Grandma went home and told everybody that Herr Schwind would help us. But I wanted to know how, and went to bed disheartened.

We leave for Eisenach

After a few days the doorbell rang. Who could it be at this time in the morning? When I opened the door Herr Schwind stood there. I shouted to my mother: "Mother! Herr Schwind is here!" My mother came at once and asked Otto if there was any news.

"Of course, Frau Schumann, sit down. I have good news."

"Really?"

"I have organised an apartment for you, but it is a long way from here! It is in a town called Eisenach, in Thuringia in the east of the country, but very peaceful. I am sure you and your children will like it there. I'll give you the name of the lady who will meet you at the station. Her name is Frau Mueller, she is plump, with a small build, and she will take you to the apartment. She will be expecting you three days from now. I will give you the date and time to leave, and tell you when the train is due."

'Oh, that is fantastic, Otto, thank you so much for all your help"

He said: "Start packing, folks," and closed the door behind him.

Mother said: "This is really good news. Let's get packing, but only the essentials, children. We will all go to grandma and grandpa to tell them the good news and to say goodbye. We will take you to the station."

When the day came we were off to the station to catch our train. We embraced and kissed, and hoped it would not be for the last time. They wished us luck with our venture to a new home. We boarded the train and waved until it disappeared into the distance. We could not control our tears. The train rolled on and on, in and out of station after station, passing through desolate countryside strewn with wrecked and abandoned military and civilian hardware, through villages and towns. Then all of a sudden we saw lovely countryside and we knew that we would soon be at our destination.

Finally we arrived after a long and exhausting journey. We got off the train and fought our way out of the station, then we saw a plump little lady, seemingly waiting for us. She came up to us smiling and called out: "Are you Frau Schumann?"

"Yes, and you must be Frau Mueller, right?"

"Come with me," she said, laughing, "I will take you to your place. I have a little car, a Trabant."

My mother was still worried and hoped not to be betrayed, although she was an Aryan. For us kids it was all exciting.

Volkschule

Once settled, my mother had to make arrangements for us to attend primary school, called *Volkschule*, after which pupils had to sit an exam in order to qualify for high school. The school was a long way from our apartment, all the way up a steep hill. And in those days we didn't have the facility of catching a bus or a tram.

I settled in well and made friends with Edith. We spent a lot of time together, walking, hiking, roller skating and playing tennis. We would also invite each other for cake and a refreshing drink in the afternoons. I also made the acquaintance of Anni, called Anneliese by the teachers in their strict way. Most of the teachers were middle-aged, just one or two seemed younger. Anni had a sister called Jutta. She was older and already in high school. Sometimes she would join us, but she had her own interests. Their father had a confectionery shop.

We started school at 7 o'clock in the morning and finished at 1pm. On Saturdays we started at 8 and finished at 12 pm. We had some good times together, although a war was raging all over Europe. Sirens were introduced, which made an eerie sound and meant that we had to seek shelter in cellars. Dogs and cats were not allowed in a shelter and one could hear them howling with anxiety.

A law came out saying that girls who had reached ten years old must join the BDM (*Bund Deutscher Mädel*), the girls' wing of the Nazi Party youth movement – there was a similar organisation for boys. The outfit was a white blouse, black skirt, a mustard jacket, white socks and black shoes. To be honest I loved this outfit, and so did my friends.

We noticed one day that the confectionery shop was closed. I couldn't see Anni any more, she didn't come back to school. Nobody knew where Anni and Jutta had gone and we missed them.

After that Edith and I spent as much time together as we could. This was the end of 1943 when everything was rationed, including fuel. Winter arrived with icy cold weather and it was hard to reach school, although it was nearer now than before.

Allied bombing

My grandmother wrote frequently and told my mother what was going on in Berlin with its endless bombing. She hoped we were safe and also told us how lucky we were not to be there!

The allied bombing was continuing and Christmas 1943 was not a happy time since we did not have enough food, but Edith helped us out many times. Her parents owned a restaurant and so she had access to some food. She was a really good friend.

New Year arrived and people celebrated as much as they could. The year 1944 was not much better. We got used to the situation and the thunder of foreign planes heading in the direction of Berlin, there must have been thousands.

My father arrives in Eisenach

At last the year 1945 arrived, and after a lovely spring, summer finally greeted us with warm sunshine. But my mother was very upset since she hadn't heard anything from her parents. She kept saying, "I hope their house will not be bombed." We heard the noise of gunshots from far away and the ground shook under our feet. We knew the war must be ending, but one did not dare mention this.

The weeks went by and my mother was just hanging some washing on the line when a man walked up the hill leading to our house. He looked very tired and was dressed in shabby clothes. My mother turned and was just saying something to this old man when he came closer and said, "It's me, Anna, your husband!"

"Oh my God" she whispered with shock, "you have come back to us, love."

And then they embraced.

I came running out of the house and embraced him too.

"Where is Rudi, Anna?"

"Oh don't worry, he is visiting a friend. We are all well and survived this war, up to now. Come inside, love, have a rest and I'll make you something to eat. How did you know we had moved up here?"

"I'll tell you later how I found out… the main thing is we are together now."

The Americans in Thuringia

During the weeks of American occupation of Thuringia at the end of the war in summer 1945, in Eisenach we were all treated well and with respect. After my father's return we were once again a happy family. As before, I visited my friend Edith quite often and we went to the tennis court frequently, or did some hiking. She was always pleased to see me. On one occasion when I went to visit her, when I entered the hotel there were many Americans running about, always happy and singing or whistling. I asked Edith's father, "Where is Edith? I can't find her." He said, "Go to the back where she is playing on her piano."

So I went straight away where I found her at the piano, but she was crying.

"Whatever is the matter, Edith? Please tell me, who has upset you?"

She turned to me, glad I came to see her, and told me that one of the Americans approached her this morning to tell her that they had to leave the town very soon. And he gave her the news that the whole of Thuringia would now fall within the Soviet occupation zone. He advised her to leave as soon as possible, but this was not so easy.

Then to her surprise Anni came to see her, and told her the whole story about how she had returned from a camp and was delighted to be welcomed by the Americans. However, Edith told Anni that times were going to change because the Americans had to leave town.

This was not expected at all and Anni asked "What happens when they have gone?"

"We will have a Russian occupation, of course," Lottie replied. "And I really have missed you, Anni. Sit down and tell us what happened when you were absent."

I went home that day to tell my parents the news. They got straight in touch with my grandparents, who lived in the west zone of Berlin, who asked us to leave and come to live with them.

One early morning on 1st July 1945, Russian troops marched through the gates of Eisenach. We left just in time. I remember how upset my friends were when I bid goodbye. They thought it was the last time. This was a sad day for all of us.

We move back to Berlin

My grandparents were already waiting for us when we got off the train. At first we didn't see them because there were so many people going to and fro. But then they pushed through the crowds and embraced us. Granddad said, "You made the right decision to come to the West, but we are sorry you had to give up the nice place where you spent the war years."

Mother then said, "We worried about you with all the bombing and hoped your apartment would not be destroyed. You were lucky!" We all went to their home and were so happy to be together again, after such a long time.

My grandparents said, "We also worried about you. But first you must eat and tomorrow you can tell us everything that happened." We were shown to our sleeping arrangements which were cosy. At first I was upset having to leave my dear friends in Eisenach, but soon I fell asleep. I woke up to a beautiful day, with sunshine streaming into my bedroom. I was happy again, especially knowing that my parents had found each other again after so many years.

The following day our grandparents told us that we could stay with them until we found other accommodation, which they said could take a long time, since 600,000 apartments had been destroyed and only 2.8 million of the city's original population of 4.3 million still lived in the city. Also food had become short, and medicines too. Granddad said, "We thought we would make all that clear to you, just in case you think it is better here." However, we were in the West Zone, thank God!

We were grateful for the information since we had no idea about life in Berlin, but we knew it would not be easy. My father was able to get his former job back as a lawyer. His associate and friend had retired so he had to get used to new staff, but he said that they were very friendly to work with. My mother also tried to get a job, but this was not easy at all. She went to the job centre and explained that she used to be a shorthand typist. "Come back in a few months", the assistant told her. She had already queued for an hour and was annoyed because the assistant didn't show any interest or provide any help. "Next please!", she shouted.

I thought that maybe, since I was only 16, I would have a better chance, but weeks went by with no job. Since I wanted to earn my keep, I helped with the housework and shopping, and got part-time work in a grocery shop. Somehow we all managed, using the money which dad earned as a lawyer for our upkeep. Our grandparents were very understanding and never grumbled. There was never an argument and we all lived in harmony.

Every night, after my dad came home from work, we used to sit together for our evening meal. My dad turned the radio on to listen to the news or to music. In those days not many people owned a radio. It was a luxury. I helped my mother with the dishes, and afterwards we all settled down. My grandmother used to knit. She loved knitting and made some fantastic knitwear in her time. It was very cosy: the clock was ticking and their beloved dog lay stretched out on the rug, near the fire.

But then horror struck.

Rape

At the end of the war, after the Battle of Berlin in 1945, Soviet soldiers started raping women on a huge scale.

I recall what happened one morning when I saw lorries loaded with Russian soldiers. They jumped off the lorries and ran into every house where women lived. They were shouting and laughing. They hadn't yet made their way to our house. Mother called to me, "Come away from the window, Lottie." Frau Molke lived across the road from us and she had two teenage girls who were vulnerable due to their age at that time. Because of this Frau Molke was really anxious about what could happen to them. Fortunately they didn't enter her house, but that wasn't to say that it wouldn't happen on another day. The following day a lorry of soldiers arrived again on our street. This time they came to our door and banged loudly, shouting in Russian which we could not understand. My mother said: "I am going to open the door, because if I don't they will break in one way or the other."

The banging continued and when my mother opened the door the two soldiers very rudely entered our front room. This time they didn't seem interested in us, because they had their beady eyes on some items of value. They kicked my grandmothers' china cabinet and grabbed some valuable items, like a small silver vase and some silver plates. One soldier grabbed some silver cutlery, the other ordered my granddad to give him his watch. He had no other choice but to give it to him. They both went and we were relieved, because there was no rape.

The following day they came back on their lorry, this time drunk. My mother urged me to hide: "Quickly, get under the bed". However, they didn't come to our house on this occasion.

Later that evening Frau Molke came to our house and she was crying.

"Come in, love, what is the matter? Did anything happen?"

"Yes, it did, you wouldn't believe it, because yesterday one soldier stormed into our house. I had to open the door, you know, otherwise they would have broken it in. But all at once another came after him. They got hold of one of my daughters and fondled her, but she struggled and screamed. I tried to help, but the other one got hold of me too. All of us were raped that morning."

"I am so sorry, Frau Molke. What can we do? Sit down, love. There must be something we can do."

One morning I went shopping. Because of the long queues I thought I couldn't stand on my feet any longer. Again I saw the long queue before me. People were all talking about what happened in the last few days. "There have been a lot of rapes recently, you know." They talked in a low voice, but I could still hear them.

"Excuse me, where did this happen?" I asked. They told me and warned me to be careful. At last it was my turn, but I got only a few potatoes, sugar and a cabbage. They told me they had sold out of butter. "Come back tomorrow!" There was never enough food for all of us. How lucky we were because my grandmother and my mother knew how to economise.

It was November now and we were huddled together near the fire, when an urgent knock on the door suddenly upset our peaceful evening. My mother was surprised to find my dad's aunt on the door step.

"Do come in. It is so nice to see you. It must have been a few years now since we had some good times together." Then she said, "I have heard about the rape going on in the city and I was concerned about Lottie"

"Up to now, we have been lucky but a few neighbours have not been lucky at all, since their daughters were raped the other day. We only hope they don't come back here again."

"Yes, well, that is why I came to see you. Since we have a farm in the country it would be safer for Lottie to stay with us for a while. Of course you can come as well. You are still youngish and the Russians might get hold of you as well."

"This has come so suddenly, we must think about it since we would have to leave grandma and papa on their own."

"Yes, but your husband could help, I thought he came home every night from his job."

"It is a good idea, but what will our Lottie do on a farm?"

"She can help us and we know she will at least be safe from these Russians."

"You can stay for the night and we will discuss this in the morning," suggested my grandma.

The following day they all agreed it would be a good idea for me to live with my aunt. I was so happy that I would be able to get away from there! My mother helped me to pack a few essentials in a large case. But that same evening tragedy struck. Banging on our door again. Clearly this was not a neighbour, no neighbour would bang on our door like this. My mother said, "I have a bad feeling that these are Russians again. Hide under the bed and try to be still, Lottie." My mother was right. Two Russians walked drunkenly into our front room. Some Russians understood the language. "Wo ist schoenes fraulein?" meaning: "Where is the pretty miss?"

"She is not here", my mother tried to explain.

They started to search and looking under the bed they found me. It's too late, I thought, I should have left last night with aunty. They reeked of alcohol and one grabbed me with his dirty hands. They dragged me out and threw me on the bed. My family stood there helplessly, but tried to drag the soldier from me. I screamed and the other one slapped me in the face and exercised his pleasure on me too. They left me crying and helpless on the floor. Then they left.

Escape to Dahlem Dorf

My father advised to leave at once. I was still dazed from the cruelty of these soldiers, but my mother and father comforted me as best as they could. It was upsetting to leave my grandma and grandpapa behind. We embraced each other a long time until it was time to leave. My father took us in his Trabant.

"Where are we going and what is the place called, Papa?"

"I'm sorry. I didn't have much time to explain where we are going. It is a village called Dahlem Dorf on the outskirts of Berlin. You will like the village and also the farm."

"Oh, I hope so dad. All this will be very strange to me, but at last I will find safety with your relatives."

It was now December 1945 and there was a sharp breeze and gradually snow was falling, covering the endless fields and little farmhouses. Eventually, when the light was fading, we arrived at our destination. Slipping and sliding we made our way to the front door where everybody was already waiting. "Come in, all of you. It's freezing out there." It was six days before Christmas and I stared in disbelief when I saw a huge Christmas tree, decorated with glass balls and ornaments and tinsel.

"How was your journey, Fred?"

"We are very glad to have arrived without any mishaps, Julie. I must say I like your tree. So beautifully decorated!"

"Fred you must stay the night, because the roads are not safe at night."

"Of course dear, but I must leave early tomorrow to reach my office. Come Lottie, we'll have our supper now and afterwards you can tell us anything you want us to hear."

My dad left the following day and promised to keep in touch with us. He got in his Trabant and made his way towards Berlin.

Christmas 1945 finally arrived. There was a lot to do since chickens needed feeding, and we needed to make sure the horses were looked after and made safe for the night. The sheep were also well tended. I had a present for my aunt, a warm cardigan which my grandma knitted on those lonely nights. She was overjoyed. They had some chocolates for me and a shawl which was colourful and very warm! We sang Christmas songs and played a few games. I was not used to these games, but soon they taught me.

Christmas went and New Year 1946 arrived with heavy snowfalls. This meant they had to fetch the sheep inside for warmth and safety. In the mornings I always collected the eggs from a secure hut where the chickens were kept overnight. My mother helped also, but I got the lighter jobs. In the evenings we would sit in front of the television and a blazing log fire. Nobody bothered us. It was so peaceful. I had to think about my future, but while the cold war was still raging I could not make any plans.

We all made the best of it. I was only too glad to be away from the city and away from the fear of Russian soldiers arriving daily to our house and other people's properties. We all worked together. Mother helped Franz, and aunty did the housework, cleaning, cooking and baking. She would often bake bread, and the aroma filled the whole house. At the weekends she would bake cakes and buns. We were lucky to have all those ingredients available. There was a henhouse on the far side of the garden where chickens were kept in order to supply the family with fresh laid eggs. I was in charge of this and enjoyed my work, and liked it that everybody was aware of my help. We also had two jersey cows which supplied us with our daily milk.

Alexander

After a few weeks I began to feel faint and started to vomit. I didn't think it was much, thinking that I had just eaten too much, but this carried on daily until my mother noticed something was amiss.

"Lottie", she said with great concern, "I think we ought to go to the doctor to find out if there is anything wrong with you."

"Why, mother? I am fine, and I don't have to go to the doctor." Mother and aunty insisted, and one day we went to the surgery. I thought that I had better explain that I was raped by two soldiers when living at home with my grandparents. The doctor was very understanding and listened to my story. After examining me he announced my pregnancy. I was shocked and cried. "Doctor, I can't have this baby you must understand! I have lost my virginity to a man I have never loved!" The doctor assured me not to worry since there was nothing he could do about it. Mother and aunty put their arms around me and comforted me. "Lottie, let's go home. We will look after you."

However, I was angry and when we got back I locked myself in my bedroom and cried until there were no more tears left. Nine months later there was this tiny baby boy with dark hair and brown eyes smiling up at me as I cradled him in my arms.

They all looked after me so well bringing up Alexander. He grew up to be a nice loving boy who had our loving family around him. He did well in school and, at that time, he had to help on the farm because he could not venture into the city.

Berlin Airlift

A few years after the end of the war (this was in 1948-49) we heard about the Berlin Airlift. The United States of America had begun a massive airlift of food, water and medicines to the citizens of the besieged city of Berlin. This was in response to the Berlin blockade, which lasted for 318 days when the Soviet Union refused to allow the Allies to carry supplies by land to the inhabitants of West Berlin. Supplies from American planes would sustain over a million people in West Berlin. The blockade ended in spring 1949. People said that Stalin was powerless to stop the airlift, because he could not shoot down those planes, as it would have provoked a World War.

Life in Berlin after the Airlift

We heard that my granddad in Berlin had become ill. My grandmother worried and hoped it would not be anything too serious. We were told that it was a very bad flu, and it was getting worse, but luckily he was able to get treatment, thanks to the Americans who helped with supplies of medicines. Then he got all the care he needed from my grandmother and soon he felt better. Also my grandparents had good neighbours who were concerned about my granddad's health.

It was now August in Berlin, there was some lovely weather and it was even possible for people to forget about all the ruins that surrounded them.

Then one day people got ration cards. They were meagre rations but people had to put up with them. Frau Mueller would often visit my grandparents during these times and over a cup of coffee, which was a luxury in those days, maybe with some cake which my grandmother baked, they would have a cosy chat.

It was said that in the eastern part of the city German communists were spying on people if anything was said against the communist regime, so they would only ever speak in whispers. Weeks went by, months went by. The colder season was not far away, and the winter was dreaded because fuel was so hard to get.

Because of food shortages, there were long queues of people outside shops. Greens, oranges and bananas were luxuries and it was only the privileged few who were able to obtain these. When you were in a queue you could not be sure what you would be buying at the end of it. You would be lucky to get a loaf, margarine and a few potatoes. The food items in any one shop could vary from day to day, and sometimes there would be nothing at all. It was all very chaotic.

My father comes to Dahlem

We had not seen our dad for a long time when suddenly he arrived on our doorstep in Dahlem.

"Dad, what a surprise to see you after such a long time! Aunty, mother come quickly. Dad has come to see us!" Breathlessly they all came running into the house, with our boy Alexander.

"You all look well, it must be the countryside!"

"Dad, can we introduce you to Alexander?"

"Oh, who is this, then, may I ask?" he said curiously. "Did you get married, Lottie?"

"No, dad, I didn't. This is my son."

"Your son?"

"Yes, dad. Years ago, when I was living at home in Berlin, I was raped by one of those Russian soldiers. But I had no choice but to go through with my pregnancy. I know it is a lot for you to take in. We could not let you know since correspondence was impossible and still is."

"I am so sorry, Lottie. But I am pleased that you are happy now."

Aunty called us. "Would everybody please come and have some supper since your dad has had a long journey and he must be very hungry now." We all sat down around the long farm table and enjoyed our meal. Alexander seemed to be a little shy, but soon we were all chatting and put him at ease. "Now, Dad, will you tell us why you have not come earlier?"

"Of course, my dears. After supper, when we are all relaxing near such a lovely fire, I will tell you the latest."

"I tried several times setting off to visit you, but every time I was followed by a black car. I had a bad feeling that they were *Volkspolizei*, probably wanting to spy on me and where I was going. The first time I was heading towards Dahlem, and the car was still behind me. I changed my mind then and turned in a different direction towards a public house. I got out and went for a drink of beer and sat down near a window where I could see anybody approaching. Then, two men got out of their car and entered the pub as well. They ordered their drink and joked with the barman, then sat down and eyed me up and down. I decided that when I finished my drink I should go back home. After a while, however, this black car was following me again, until I arrived home. I thought it might have just been a coincidence. When I arrived home my parents were intrigued by what I told them. I was busy at the office for a few days, but I wanted to try again to see you. It is hard for me, love, that we have to live apart for so long."

He said all this to his loving wife and she said, "I understand, love. It will not to be forever."

Then he carried on with his tale. "The second time I travelled again towards the village, and would you believe it, they followed me again. Honestly, I was getting a bit scared by then. I turned back and tried to find another pub. This time I didn't see them and walked into a quaint looking pub. I didn't stay long and was walking towards my car when I saw the same black car again. These two men stopped me and asked me if I would like to join them for a drink. I said, "Really, I have to go back to my parents," but they insisted and therefore I agreed to have a drink with them. They started asking questions about where I live and if I have any children, but I didn't tell them anything. They seemed to be satisfied. Later I called to them in the car park: "You do a good job, comrades, keep it up!" You see they thought I was on their side. Now on my third try I have come to you without any mishap."

"You will stay tonight or must you rush off again?" asked my mother.

"Of course I will stay for a night, and tomorrow, I hope, it will be the last time that you all have to wait for me for such a long time. But who knows."

After we all had our breakfast it was time Papa had to leave us. We gathered outside and embraced. My eyes were damp with tears. He also said to us. "I like Alexander, he seems to be a nice lad."

As started to rev up his car we called out: "See you soon, Papa. We love you and thanks for coming!"

Somehow the place seemed to be so empty and still after he left. After that, weeks, months and years went by, then one day, Franz, aunty's husband, suddenly fell ill. Mother fetched the doctor, but it was too late, he died of a heart attack. Sadly he would never experience the fall of the wall in Berlin.

In 1975 Alexander got married. We tried to give him the best wedding day and a great feast. By 1977 the couple had two lovely children, a girl and a boy. Alexander decided to stay on the farm to work and look after my aunt.

The Wall goes up

It was reported that one night in 1961, people in Berlin woke up suddenly to the noise of heavy machinery. East German police and Soviet troops were pulling up tracks and roads. They were all helping to erect barriers, topped with barbed wire. My father said that this was very bad news, it looked like they were going to build a concrete wall between East and West Berlin. Frau Mueller was very worried, but at first my father thought that they shouldn't be too concerned because they were in the western part of the city.

But then something unbelievable happened. There were some apartment buildings whose doors faced east, while the back windows ran along a West Berlin street. One of the German East *Volkspolizei* came to all the apartments on our street to inform us that these apartments were facing to the east now.

He said: "I hope you are aware you won't live in the west part of Berlin any more. From now on you live in the east sector of Berlin. You are not allowed to cross to the other side."

"Well, that is not fair. Our relatives live there. You must realise that, Herr policeman?"

"You don't argue with me, my lady, I hope you follow the instructions I have given to you. And by the way, you can't go back to your jobs. They are on the other side of the border now, therefore don't try to cross it!" Then he went.

Frau Mueller came running across and said, through her tears, "Have you heard the news? That policeman was full of authority and made it clear to us that we are living in the DDR now."

"Of course, Frau Mueller we have to accept this, as we can't do anything about it."

One night when my father came home from work, he explained that they would have to be very careful from now on, that there would be two walls, measuring 155 kilometres, 12 feet tall, lined with 302 watchtowers with heavily armed guards. These walls were separated by a heavily guarded mined corridor, a corridor that came to be known as the death strip. Many would try to escape from the East, but sadly most of them would lose their lives.

The Wall comes down

One evening many years later, in 1989, we were all gathered around the television in Dahlem. I went into the kitchen to put the kettle on, got cups and plates our for biscuits when aunty called out to us with delight: "Lottie, come here quick, something happened. Look, the wall has come down, look at all these people laughing and screaming with joy."

"Oh how wonderful. That means we can go home now, mother!"

This was the best news we ever had. The news was announced on 9th November, 1989. It was the greatest event in our history, which marked the fall of the iron curtain and the start of the fall of communism in Eastern and Central Europe. The most symbolic breakthrough in the wall occurred at Potsdam Platz, the very centre of the old Berlin before partition. On that day the mayors of the two Berlins, Walter Homper and Ehrhard Krack, met at Potsdam Platz and shook hands, sealing officially the end of the wall which divided their city for so long.

We return to our grandparents

The day came when my mother and I prepared for our journey home. Papa came to fetch us in his Brabant. Aunty gave us some eggs, butter, flour and a jug of delicious cow's milk. She waved us off but we knew that from now on we would be seeing each other often.

Finally we arrived home and were greeted and embraced by my grandparents. "You do look well, I must say, and it is so nice to see you again at last! First of all you must have something to eat!" Grandma was delighted with all those provisions from aunty.

"Food was getting shorter each day and people still tried to escape," she told us. "Some were successful, some got caught and some got shot. It's been terrible here, but thank God it's all over now! Lottie, your dad filled me in on your life. I am glad it all turned out for the good. I hope I will see your son Alexander one day. It was not his fault or yours. I heard that after the first wave of euphoria many people returned to their houses in the East, but approximately 100,000 stayed in the west. "All this has brought me so much grief and misery over the last forty years," she said.

The following day I tried to get some work, of any kind, but nothing was available, since the younger ones were the ones who were entitled to work. I was now nearing the age when I was not needed. When I came back from my walks I noticed people looked happier, and people came from abroad to see the Wall dismantled and some kept pieces as souvenirs!

A letter from Edith

One morning my grandma called out: "Lottie, there is a letter for you!" I ran into the front room and was amazed to see that it was a letter from Anni, who had had been living in England since 1951. I sat down and eagerly read it. She said that she was coming to Germany to visit Edith in Eisenach and asked if I would also like to join them for this occasion. I told everybody about this letter, they were very pleased for me and urged me to write back straight away. I sat down that very evening and wrote a letter to Edith to say that I would come. I asked her to just let me know the date and place and I would meet them both.

Finally I got a reply from Edith giving me the date and place. We were all very excited when the big day came. My mother took me to the railway station and made sure I got on the right train. Slowly it came into sight and pulled in, passengers poured out and smoke hung in the air.

I got on and found a nice seat near a window, where I could see my mother waving to me. "Have a good time, Lottie!" she shouted when the train set in motion.

The trains ran much slower in those days and it took a while before I got to my destination. I got off eagerly and with much haste, struggling with my suitcase, wondering if everything would turn out well.

Arriving in Eisenach

I walked through the crowds where people were arriving and leaving, some meeting friends, others were business people. Then I heard the whistle for my train to leave again, and after that everything went quiet. I was standing on the platform waiting for my friend, looking around in all directions, when the station master saw me in distress.

"Are you all right? Are you waiting for someone?" he asked politely.

"Yes, I am waiting for a friend," I said in an irritated voice. "She should be here by now, and I have come from Berlin."

He was very helpful and understanding and suggested to wait a little longer, and took me to the stationmaster's place where he offered me a drink. Then we saw somebody running and waving. I thanked the stationmaster profusely for his help, and he said, "I'm glad you found each other, have a good time," and walked back with a big smile on his face.

Edith said, "I am so sorry but the bus was delayed, please forgive me that you had to wait a long time."

"But where is Anni?"

"She is coming tomorrow because her plane was delayed too."

"Never mind, let's go to my flat now and tomorrow we'll meet her at the same place."

The following day we made our way to the station and waited for her on the platform.

"Hello!" she shouted, and came running towards us.

We walked away from the station arm in arm and headed towards Edith's flat, which was really nice and comfortable. A meal was already prepared which we all enjoyed. After that we gathered round the table and each of us told our story of gruesome times. We had been through so much. And we said to each other, "It was so nice that the three of us could meet again. Let's hope that nothing like that will ever happen again."

Epilogue by Anni

After a few weeks we had to leave. First it was Lottie who had to catch a train to Berlin. We all embraced and hoped that it would not be the last time. With tears in our eyes we embraced again, wishing Lottie all the best and a pleasant journey back. The train arrived early and Edith and I made sure that Lottie got a good seat where we could see her and wave to her.

We ran alongside the train and shouted, "Don't forget to write!" but because of the screeching noise and smoke she would not have heard us, and that left us both quite upset.

Now we had to wait for my train to Frankfurt, where I would catch a plane to England. Edith and I chatted for a while, with people around us shouting, laughing, crying, maybe looking for relatives or friends to be united with again. All at once we heard the announcement that my train was due at any moment. We embraced and promised to write to each other if possible. The sound of the whistle meant the train was about to depart. Slowly I moved away from my friend, leaving her sad and lonely, until the train got smaller and smaller for her and vanished into the distance.

Later I was able to visit Edith, in fact a few times, and twice with my husband. Since then we have been writing to each other regularly. We are both now very old, but still well at the age of 94. Sadly my dear husband passed away, and neither Edith nor I have heard anything again from Lottie.

I thought about how our lives had changed, yet the three of us were able to live, to survive and to thrive. I reflected that we must find patience in our lives and trust God to lead us where we need to go.

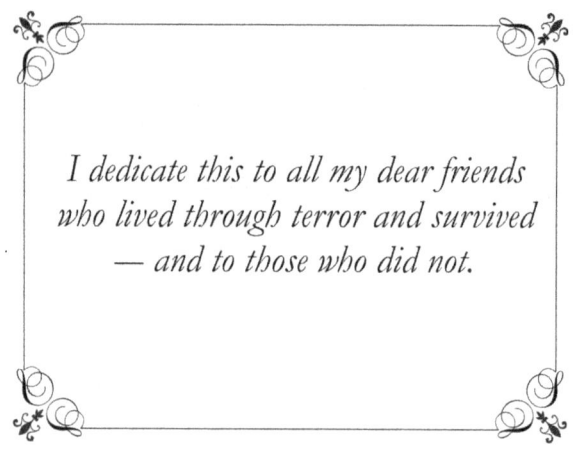

I dedicate this to all my dear friends who lived through terror and survived — and to those who did not.

www.ingramcontent.com/pod-product-compliance
Lightning Source LLC
Chambersburg PA
CBHW052134110526
44591CB00012B/1716